Judicious Choices

JUDICIOUS CHOICES

The New Politics of
Supreme Court Confirmations

Mark Silverstein

W·W·Norton & Company · New York · London

The text of this book is composed in Palatino
Compostion by ComCom
Manufacturing by Haddon Craftsmen
Book design by Yor Ffodet

Library of Congress Cataloging-in-Publication Data
Silverstein, Mark, 1947–
Judicious choices : the new politics of the Supreme Court
confirmations / Mark Silverstein. — 1st ed.
    p.   cm.
Includes bibliographical references and index.
1. Judges—Selection and appointment—United States—History.
2. United States Supreme Court—Officials and
employees—Selection and appointment—History.   I. Title.
KF8776.S55   1994
347.73'14—dc20
[347.30714]   94-1619

ISBN 0-393-03692-8

W. W. Norton & Company, Inc.,
500 Fifth Avenue, New York, N.Y. 10110
W. W. Norton & Company Ltd.,
10 Coptic Street, London WC1A 1PU

1   2   3   4   5   6   7   8   9   0

For Aline

"It is not easy to conceive a plan better calculated than this to promote a judicious choice of men for filling the offices of the Union."

—*The Federalist* No. 76

CONTENTS

Judicious Choices

INTRODUCTION: A NEW POLITICS OF JUDICIAL CONFIRMATIONS

In January of 1932 Justice Oliver Wendell Holmes, at the age of ninety-two, announced his retirement from the Supreme Court, after thirty years of distinguished service. Among the names quickly surfacing as a possible replacement for the legendary Holmes was Benjamin Cardozo, a Democrat and the respected chief judge of the New York Court of Appeals. During his years on New York's highest state court, Cardozo had established a national reputation as a progressive jurist and as author of the classic *The Nature of the Judicial Process*.[1] The nomination of Cardozo, however, presented President Herbert Hoover with several difficulties. The president was facing the prospect of a tough reelection battle, and the choice of a Democrat was certain to anger many in Hoover's Republican party. Cardozo's appointment, moreover, would bring a third New Yorker and a second Jew to the Court. One did not have to be an anti-Semite to maintain that the president might rightfully seek greater diversity on the Court. Finally, Cardozo's reputation as a progressive was firmly established, and there was little doubt that he would join with Brandeis and Stone on the "liberal" wing of the Court. In sum, there was precious little political gain for Hoover in a Cardozo appointment.

Politics aside, however, there was much to recommend Cardozo.

---

1. One measure of Cardozo's influence may lie in the fact that *The Nature of the Judicial Process*, first published in 1921, sold over 170,000 copies through 1989 and continues to be found on the reading list in undergraduate and law school classes studying the process of judicial decision making.

The stature of the nominee was of paramount importance. Cardozo was a highly distinguished jurist, and Hoover was conscious of the potential ignominy in being remembered by history as the president who filled the Holmes seat on the Court with an unknown. Although a Republican, Hoover was inclined to name a Democrat, if only to be faithful to his personal belief that appointments to the Court must be nonpartisan. Prior to making a final decision, Hoover received a visit from Senator William Borah, the powerful Republican senator from Idaho. Borah championed Cardozo as the best candidate regardless of residence, religion, or party affiliation and strongly hinted to Hoover that the Senate would resist unknown candidates on the grounds of "obscurity." Cardozo's nomination followed almost immediately, and he cleared the Senate without dissent or discussion. A few days later Hoover wrote a prominent Republican that the choice of Cardozo "was a difficult matter from many points of view. It contains more political liabilities than assets but I felt that I must disregard such questions."[2]

To the modern student of American politics, the story of Cardozo's appointment to the Court must appear as a wondrous fable of a land far away and a time long ago. It is difficult, if not impossible, to imagine prominent members of one political party today championing the nomination of a member of the opposition to the Supreme Court, and the notion that a president might be constrained to seek only nominees of stature and prominence is simply too fanciful to be seriously entertained. That a Democratic nominee with the long public career and the controversial publications of a Cardozo could be nominated by a Republican president and confirmed by a voice vote of a Republican-controlled Senate, all within a period of ten days, is itself beyond modern comprehension.

Equally startling, perhaps, is the fact that from the turn of the century through 1967 only one nominee—John J. Parker in 1930—

---

2. Quoted in Andrew Kaufman, "Cardozo's Appointment to the Supreme Court," *Cardozo Law Review* 1 (1979): 23. Much of the material concerning the Cardozo appointment is drawn from Professor Kaufman's article.

out of a total of forty-three failed to gain Senate approval. The defeat of Parker, in spite of Republican control of both the White House and the Senate, came as a surprise and in a sense was a product of the same forces that produced the famous Court-packing controversy seven years later. Liberal Democrats and progressive Republicans, frustrated with a conservative Supreme Court that often denied the elected branches the constitutional authority to regulate capital, joined forces with labor and the NAACP to deny Parker confirmation.[3] Fourteen years earlier, in 1916, the nomination of Louis Brandeis had produced a bitter and far more divisive confirmation battle. The business community, united against the famous "people's attorney," mounted a furious four-month campaign to deny confirmation, based in large measure on Brandeis's "radical" beliefs on the distribution of wealth in America. Seven former presidents of the American Bar Association signed a public statement proclaiming Brandeis "unfit" to sit on the Supreme Court. Beneath the surface of the debate over political and judicial philosophy lay a virulent strain of anti-Semitism. Nonetheless, despite this most determined opposition, Brandeis was eventually confirmed by a rather comfortable margin.

The defeat of Parker and the bitter battle over Brandeis represented the extraordinary; for almost seventy years the confirmation process was distinguished by a strong presumption in favor of deference to presidential prerogative to fill vacancies on the Supreme Court.[4] A president could be expected to seek counsel from diverse sources both in and out of government, and part of the process might

3. Three months earlier, Charles Evans Hughes had been confirmed as chief justice with a surprising amount of opposition because of his links with Wall Street. Parker was a far weaker candidate for the Court, and his civil rights record galvanized the opposition of the NAACP. For an interesting study asserting that the defeat of Parker was an important stage in the development of the NAACP, see Kenneth Goings, *The NAACP Comes of Age: The Defeat of Judge John J. Parker* (Bloomington: Indiana Univ. Press, 1990).

4. This presumption did not exist in the nineteenth century, when one out of every three nominees to the Court was rejected by the Senate. With senators appointed by state legislatures—the Seventeenth Amendment was ratified in 1913—powerful state party leaders were often sent to the Senate to funnel patronage back to the party organization. In an age of relatively strong party politics, simple partisan political considerations undercut any notion of deference to presidential appointments to the Court.

at times require behind-the-scenes deals to guarantee the necessary support of key Senate elders. As long, however, as the nominee exhibited a basic level of competence and his political views fit within the narrow confines of acceptable American political discourse (which is why interests seeking to deny confirmation to nominees as different as Louis Brandeis and Robert Bork inevitably characterize the nominee as "radical"), the president's choice was typically confirmed by a voice vote, with no opposition on record. From 1945 through 1967 not one nominee excited the opposition of even one-fifth of the Senate, and, when a recorded vote was taken, the opposition was token, averaging a mere twelve votes.

In 1968 the politics of judicial confirmations underwent an abrupt transformation, and the presumption respecting presidential control was honored more in the breach than in the observance. Seven of the last fifteen nominations to the Court have produced more than twenty-five negative votes in the Senate, and four nominees have been rejected.[5] The failure of the Senate to confirm Abe Fortas in 1968 as chief justice was quickly followed by the defeats of Clement Haynsworth and G. Harrold Carswell. In 1987 the controversial Robert Bork was denied confirmation in proceedings that captured wide public attention. Before the Bork defeat President Reagan had elevated William Rehnquist to the chief justiceship but only after factious hearings and even though the new chief justice received more negative votes than any other successful nominee in the twentieth century. Rehnquist held this dubious record for a mere five years, when it was shattered by the confirmation of Clarence Thomas in proceedings that stunned a nation.

The intent of this book is to provide the reader with an appreciation of the evolving political and legal contexts in which the transition from the politics of acquiescence to the politics of confrontation has taken place. Studies of judicial nominations and confirmations typically take a somewhat narrower approach to the subject. Re-

---

5. I count Abe Fortas in 1968 as a rejected nominee although, as chapter 1 indicates, his nomination was withdrawn following a failed cloture vote in the Senate.

cently, for example, several political scientists sought to construct a predictive model of judicial confirmations by isolating what are said to be critical characteristics of nominees to the Supreme Court (for instance, "ideology" and "qualifications") that are believed to influence a senator's vote.[6] Resolving that the resulting model could quite "straightforwardly" be used to predict the outcome of confirmation battles, the authors of the study conclude, "When a strong president nominates a highly qualified, ideologically moderate candidate, the nominee passes the Senate. . . . When presidents nominate a less qualified, ideologically extreme candidate, especially when the president is in a weak position, then a conflictual vote is likely."[7] My approach to the study of judicial confirmations, however, is grounded on the conviction that the measure of characteristics such as "qualifications" or even "ideology" is never static but fluctuates over time in response to the political realities of the day. The quest to construct predictive models of political behavior continues to power much political research, but, at least with respect to the selection and confirmation of Supreme Court justices, quantitative analysis that does not account for the changing political context in which judicial nominations take place is of limited usefulness to the student of politics.[8]

The principal genre for the study of judicial confirmations has been the case study. The selection of a Supreme Court justice often gives rise to weighty political drama and has generated, particularly in recent years, a fair share of insider accounts.[9] This micro-analysis

6. See Charles Cameron, Albert Cover, and Jeffrey Segal, "Senate Voting on Supreme Court Nominees: A Neoinstitutional Model," *American Political Science Review* 84 (1990): 525; Jeffrey Segal and Harold Spaeth, *The Supreme Court and the Attitudinal Model* (New York: Cambridge Univ. Press, 1992), chap. 4.

7. Ibid. at 532.

8. For a critique, see Mark Silverstein and William Haltom, "Can There Be a Theory of Supreme Court Confirmations?" (Paper prepared for presentation at the 1991 Annual Meeting of the Western Political Science Association, Seattle, March 21–23, 1991). For an example of a view of confirmations far more sensitive to context, see George Watson and John Stookey, "Supreme Court Confirmation Hearings: A View from the Senate," *Judicature* 71 (1988): 186.

9. Consider the following, hardly exhaustive, sample of studies of the Bork confir-

of the confirmation process reveals a wealth of valuable detail about a single nomination and, perhaps more significantly, enables the student of American government to gain important insight into the strategy and tactics of key actors in the process. At the same time, the case study may focus the reader's attention too narrowly, resulting in an unfortunate failure to appreciate the wonders of the forest while concentrating attention on a single, albeit dazzling, tree. The tension of the battle over Robert Bork, for example, or the wretched spectacle of the Clarence Thomas hearings focused our attention, but perhaps at the expense of the larger picture. The Bork and Thomas battles, I believe, cannot be considered as simply grotesque abnormalities in the traditional, business-as-usual model of judicial confirmations but instead must be examined in context as vivid examples of the evolution in the way we select and confirm Supreme Court justices.

The current process is disorderly, contentious, and unpredictable. In short, it is now a thoroughly democratic process, and the increased public participation in the selection of federal judges and Supreme Court justices is a consequence of profound changes in American politics and institutions. The most important development is the heightened activism of the modern federal judiciary.[10] Whether

---

mation battle, including a notation on the author's relationship to the proceedings: Paul Simon (senator and member of the Judiciary Committee), *Advice and Consent: Clarence Thomas, Robert Bork and the Intriguing History of the Supreme Court's Nomination Battles* (Washington, D.C.: National Press Books, 1992); Mark Gitenstein (the former chief counsel to the Judiciary Committee), *Matters of Principle: An Insider's Account of America's Rejection of Robert Bork's Nomination to the Supreme Court* (New York: Simon & Schuster, 1992); Patrick McGuigan and Dawn Weyrich (New Right activists supporting the nomination), *Ninth Justice: The Fight for Bork* (Washington, D.C.: Free Congress, 1990); Robert Bork (the nominee), *The Tempting of America: The Political Seduction of the Law* (New York: Simon & Schuster, 1990); Michael Pertschuk and Wendy Schaetzel (liberal activists opposing the nomination), *The People Rising: The Campaign against the Bork Nomination* (New York: Thunder's Mouth Press, 1989); Ethan Bronner (reporter covering the Supreme Court for the *Boston Globe*), *Battle for Justice: How the Bork Nomination Shook America* (New York: Norton, 1989).

10. When scholars speak of the "modern" judiciary, particularly the Supreme Court, they are typically refering to the Court from the New Deal to the present. I prefer a more narrow definition. In my view the "modern" era of the Supreme Court and the rest of the federal judiciary begins in 1962, with the retirement of Justice Felix Frankfurter and

one welcomes or laments the "imperial judiciary," scholars are in rare accord in their assessment that in the last thirty years the federal courts have exercised greater control over the affairs of the citizenry than previously and that the modern Supreme Court is distinguished by its readiness to strike down the acts of elected bodies.[11] Even quantifying the increasing willingness to exercise the power of judicial review fails to capture fully the extent of the changing judicial role. Since the early 1960s the federal courts have dramatically relaxed the strict rules that made access difficult and often precluded classes of issues from being raised in a federal judicial forum. Problems that only a generation or two ago would have been considered unfit for judicial resolution are now frequent subjects of litigation. Hand in hand with the disposition to entertain novel claims made by a wide range of litigants, the modern judiciary has fashioned a multitude of innovative forms of judicial relief designed to ensure compliance with court decrees by recalcitrant governmental officials. Over the last thirty years the federal judiciary has evolved to the point where it can provide litigants with relief previously available only through the executive or legislative branches.

The nature of judicial power was transformed at a time when the

---

the decision in *Baker* v. *Carr*, 369 U.S. 186 (1962). See chapter 2, for the logic underlying this conclusion.

11. The phrase "imperial judiciary" comes from the title of Nathan Glazer's oft-quoted critique of judicial activism. See Glazer, "Towards an Imperial Judiciary?" *Public Interest* Fall 1975, p. 104. For a more sympathetic treatment see Abram Chayes, "The Role of the Judge in Public Law Litigation," *Harvard Law Review* 89 (1976): 1281. "Since 1960, the Supreme Court has been striking down laws passed by Congress and the president at an average of two a year, more than double the rate of the earlier part of this century and four times the rate since 1790. The work of state and local lawmakers has fallen at a much faster rate: the Court has invalidated an average of seventeen state and local laws each year since 1960, more than four times the rate during all of the Court's previous history." David Adamany, "The Supreme Court," in John Gates and Charles Johnson, eds., *The American Courts: A Critical Assessment* (Washington, D.C.: CQ Press, 1991), p. 23. See also David O'Brien, *Storm Center: The Supreme Court in American Politics*, 2d ed. (New York: Norton, 1990), pp. 60–61; Gregory Caldeira and Donald McCrone, "Of Time and Judicial Activism: A Study of the U.S. Supreme Court, 1800–1973," in Stephen Halpern and Charles Lamb, eds., *Supreme Court Activism and Restraint* (Lexington, Mass.: Lexington Books, 1982).

coalitions governing America were in a state of flux. In chapter 3, I attempt to show how the demise of the New Deal coalition increased the importance of the federal judiciary to powerful elements in the Democratic party. Chapter 4, in turn, details how promises to recast the Supreme Court through the appointment process were a critical factor in the resurgence of the Republican party at the national level. Without a stable governing coalition, policy-making by the judiciary becomes a more pronounced feature of American politics, producing substantial conflict over the staffing of the federal courts. The impact of these developments is further magnified by changes taking place in the U.S. Senate. The "advice and consent" of the Senate is, of course, the deciding event in the confirmation of a federal judge, and chapter 5 describes the transformation of that body from a hierarchical, inner-directed chamber into a more responsive and effective institution for the articulation of group interests.

The reader is forewarned that this is not a history of contemporary confirmations to the Supreme Court. Although chapter 1 introduces the modern confirmation process by briefly relating the tale of Abe Fortas, extended discussion of the battle over Abe Fortas or even the more recent, startling proceedings on the nominations of Robert Bork and Clarence Thomas is best left to case studies or general histories of appointments to the Supreme Court.[12] The aim of this volume is to develop a greater understanding of the political and legal forces that shape the selection of nominees to the Court and the process of their confirmation.

Writing is a solitary enterprise, but bringing a manuscript to fruition is a group endeavor. Numerous friends and colleagues gave generously of their time to read and comment on portions of this book. Three deserve special mention. Professor Benjamin Ginsberg of Johns Hopkins University has been a friend and mentor since my days in graduate school, and his insights into the American political system

---

12. The best known remains Henry Abraham, *Justices and Presidents: A Political History of Appointments to the Supreme Court,* 3d ed. (New York: Oxford Univ. Press, 1992). In addition to an excellent history of each nomination to the Court, Professor Abraham provides an extensive bibliography.

pervade this work. Throughout the years I have had the good fortune in being able to collaborate with Professor William Haltom of the University of Puget Sound on several projects. I have come to rely on his astute observations regarding the American judicial system and his willingness to take time from his busy career to read and comment on my work. Finally, Roby Harrington of W. W. Norton and Company provided a level of encouragement and editorial assistance that exceeded even my wildest expectations. Without the aid and friendship of Ben, Bill, and Roby, this project would never have seen the light of day.

Portions of this book have appeared elsewhere. Prior to the Bork nomination, Ben Ginsberg and I explored the relationship of the federal courts to larger developments in the body politic in "The Supreme Court and the New Politics of Judicial Power," *Political Science Quarterly* (Fall 1987). Following the Thomas hearings, a much abbreviated outline of the ideas contained in these pages appeared in "The People, the Senate and the Court: The Democratization of the Judicial Confirmation System," *Constitutional Commentary* (Winter 1992). I have throughout what follows borrowed liberally from these pieces.

Chapter 1

THE AGONY OF ABE FORTAS

The defeat of Robert Bork's nomination to the Supreme Court in 1987 was a bitter pill for conservatives to swallow. Possessor of perhaps the most impressive résumé of any nominee since Felix Frankfurter in 1939, Bork was an outspoken critic of modern judicial activism, and his appointment, it was thought, would mark the crowning achievement in the Republican effort to transform the Supreme Court. In the months following the failed appointment, Bork toured the country. Speaking before various conservative and business groups, he asserted that his defeat was the result of the "first all-out political campaign" directed at a nominee to the Supreme Court. Conservative columnists expressed similar sentiments in the editorial pages of the nation. The Right added a new word to our political lexicon to express its displeasure: to be "Borked" was to have one's writings and opinions wrenched out of context in a well-organized campaign by opposing interests. Conservatives were unanimous in their conclusion that Bork was the first nominee in modern history denied a seat on the Court for ideological reasons. They were quite wrong in this assertion. Less than twenty years earlier, in 1968, another extraordinarily qualified nominee had fallen victim to the modern ordeal of confirmation.

THE BEST LAWYER IN AMERICA

An Extraordinary Year

In the year 1968 the world appeared to turn upside down. The anguish of the Kennedy and King assassinations merged with the searing images of the terror of the Tet offensive, the conflagration of

America's urban ghettos, the drama of the Prague Spring, the turmoil of the May events in France, and the police riot of the Chicago Democratic National Convention to produce an overwhelming sensation that the center could not possibly hold. The chasm between black and white, young and old, hawk and dove, simply appeared too great. In the same year that Dr. Benjamin Spock, the author of the best-selling *The Common Sense Book of Baby and Child Care*, was convicted of conspiring to counsel evasion of the draft, Richard Nixon arose from the dustbin of political history to become the president of the United States. Campuses from Columbia University, in New York, to Nihon University, in Tokyo, were in open revolt. Even the once tranquil world of amateur sport could not escape the politics of confrontation; the most enduring portrait of the times remains that of a defiantly clenched fist raised in a black-power salute above an Olympic awards podium.

During a time of cataclysmic events, the merely extraordinary ones often escape attention. In June of 1968, as the nation buried another Kennedy, Chief Justice Earl Warren informed President Lyndon Johnson of his plan to retire after fourteen years on the Supreme Court. Johnson quickly formulated a strategy to elevate his friend and confidant Associate Justice Abe Fortas to the chief justiceship. The president would fail in this endeavor. Johnson's fabled mastery and control of the legislative process evaporated in an astonishing series of events, culminating in the Senate's refusal to end debate on the Fortas confirmation and in the president's subsequent withdrawal of the nomination. Within weeks of the Fortas disaster, Richard Nixon made the Warren Court a central issue in his campaign for the presidency, castigating the justices for "weakening the peace forces against the criminal forces" in American society and promising upon election to bring to the Court "strict constructionists" who would presumably redress the imbalance in constitutional decision making. The theme resonated throughout the Nixon campaign; in effect, the Republican candidate for the presidency ran against both his Democratic opponent and the U.S. Supreme Court.

The summer and fall of 1968 thus marked a pivotal moment in

the history not only of the nation but of the Supreme Court as well. The Senate's failure to confirm Fortas was itself a remarkable event. Only once before in the twentieth century had the Senate blocked a nominee to the high court, and, although Johnson was a lame-duck president, there was little to suggest that the master of congressional relations would be thwarted in his attempt to name a new chief justice. Nor was Fortas an unknown outsider; only three years earlier, in a simple voice vote, the Senate had confirmed him as associate justice. The tawdry financial dealings that led to his resignation from the Court the following year were still, for the most part, hidden from public view. To even the most skeptical observer of the American political scene, the nomination of Fortas must have appeared a sure thing. To the astute observer, however, the Senate's failure to confirm signaled an important shift not only in the process of appointing Supreme Court justices but in the very nature of American politics.

"Get Me Abe Fortas"

In 1939 Lyndon Johnson arrived in the House of Representatives with his eyes on the real prize, the U.S. Senate. He first sought a Senate seat in 1941 when he challenged Texas Governor Pappy ("Pass the Biscuits") O'Daniel for the Democratic nomination. With 96 percent of the primary vote counted, Johnson held a substantial lead. When the final vote was tallied, however, Pappy had miraculously received in a few rural counties enough votes to secure the nomination.[1] Seven years later O'Daniel decided not to seek reelection, and Johnson squared off against the current governor, Coke Stevenson, for the nomination. As the vote was counted, it appeared that Stevenson was

1. In 1941 the South and Texas were still solidly Democratic; a triumph in the Democratic primary thereby assured the successful candidate victory in the following general election. Two excellent, recent biographies of Abe Fortas are now available. See Laura Kalman, *Abe Fortas: A Biography* (New Haven: Yale Univ. Press, 1990); Bruce Murphy, *Fortas: The Rise and Ruin of a Supreme Court Justice* (New York: Morrow, 1988). Together with Robert Shogan's *A Question of Judgment: The Fortas Case and the Struggle for the Supreme Court* (Indianapolis: Bobbs-Merrill, 1972), they provide the factual basis for much of this chapter.

the victor by a razor-thin margin of 114 votes. But in yet another Texas electoral miracle, 202 previously uncounted votes were found in a single ballot box in Jim Wells County. That all the newly discovered votes were for Johnson and in the same handwriting and ink raised some eyebrows, but the fact was that Johnson now had the nomination by 87 votes.

Alleging fraud, Coke Stevenson turned to the federal district court to secure an injunction preventing Johnson's name from appearing on the November ballot. Johnson turned to Abe Fortas. They had first met in 1939, Johnson a young congressman with a vision of providing his constituents electricity and flood control by means of a series of dams on the Colorado River and Fortas the brilliant general counsel to the Public Works Administration. In the following years they had become fast friends, each in effect recognizing the extraordinary talent that the other brought to his chosen career. In this moment of crisis, as Lyndon Johnson saw his dream of entering the Senate being snatched away, he called on Fortas. And Fortas did not disappoint his old friend. Working under intense time pressure, Fortas maneuvered the case before Supreme Court Justice Hugo Black, who, in his capacity as circuit justice for the Fifth Circuit, vacated the stay, thus enabling Johnson to run as the Democratic candidate in the general election. From that moment on, Johnson regarded Fortas, in the words of one of his biographers, as "the best lawyer he had ever known."[2]

Others shared that opinion. Editor in chief of the *Yale Law Review*, Fortas was offered a teaching position at Yale Law School upon graduation in 1933 and for six years commuted between New Haven and Washington, D.C., where he held several positions as one of Roosevelt's most devoted New Deal lawyers. In 1938 he resigned from Yale to work full-time with his mentor William O. Douglas at the Securities and Exchange Commission. When Douglas was nominated to the Supreme Court in 1939, Fortas went over to the Depart-

2. Kalman, *Abe Fortas*, p. 202. From that moment on, in honor of his victory over Stevenson, Johnson was to be known in Texas as Landslide Lyndon.

ment of Interior to work with Secretary Harold Ickes, eventually rising to the position of under secretary. Following Roosevelt's death, in 1945, Fortas left the public service to establish with his friend Thurman Arnold the law firm of Arnold & Fortas. The firm quickly became the model Washington law firm and Fortas the quintessential Washington lawyer. The general assessment in the legal community was that Fortas ranked among the most talented lawyers of his generation. He did not use that talent solely in the service of the rich and powerful. His commitment to public-interest law was legendary; during the 1950s his firm waged a continuing legal battle against McCarthyism, and in the 1960s Fortas's pro bono representation of Clarence Earl Gideon before the U.S. Supreme Court produced one of the Warren Court's most acclaimed decisions.[3] And through it all, he remained friend, confidant, and adviser to Lyndon B. Johnson.

Mr. Justice Fortas

When Lyndon Johnson took the oath of office following the assassination of John F. Kennedy, in November 1963, the life of Abe Fortas underwent an abrupt transformation. During LBJ's unhappy stint as vice-president, Fortas remained his personal lawyer but had little to do with matters of high policy at the White House. In the initial months of the Johnson presidency, however, Fortas was in daily contact with the new president. Although he continued in private law practice, Fortas was Johnson's most trusted adviser, directly consulted and involved in every major political decision.[4] Johnson planned to make his friend a part of the administration; when Attorney General

3. *Gideon v. Wainwright*, 372 U.S. 335 (1963), establishing a right to counsel for indigent defendants in felony cases. See also Anthony Lewis, *Gideon's Trumpet* (New York: Vintage, 1964).
4. "There seemed to be no subject beyond Fortas's competence. He spoke about foreign policy with Ambassador W. Averell Harriman, disagreed with the Treasury Department over a plan to have banks pay interest on government deposits, suggested a way to present a planned Defense Department cost-consciousness program to the press, and drafted a six-point memo filled with mathematical calculations on how to reduce the funds required for foreign aid appropriations by subsidizing loans from the Export-Import Bank." Murphy, *Fortas*, p. 126.

Robert Kennedy resigned during the summer of 1964 to run for a U.S. Senate seat, Johnson pressured Fortas to head the Justice Department. Fortas declined, asserting among other things that accepting an official position in the cabinet would limit the reach of services he could provide the president. Lyndon Johnson, however, was not a man who was easily denied. During the summer of 1965, when news reached the president that United Nations Ambassador Adlai Stevenson had died, Johnson persuaded Justice Arthur Goldberg to leave the Court and assume the post. To replace Goldberg, Johnson thought only of his friend Abe Fortas.

Johnson's initial task was to talk Fortas into taking the job. In 1965 Abe Fortas was at the top of his profession. His law firm—Arnold, Fortas and Porter—was flourishing, and his income (when combined with that of his wife, Carolyn Agger, a partner in the firm) was over $300,000, a spectacular sum in 1965. His lifestyle was grand, and, as a private citizen, he could serve the president while maintaining his professional independence. A seat on the Supreme Court was a temptation, but Fortas, at least outwardly, resisted and initially turned the offer down. Later Johnson enjoyed recounting how he subsequently invited Fortas to the White House to be present for an important announcement concerning troop buildups in Vietnam. On the way to the press conference, the president told Fortas he also was about to announce his nomination to the Court. Johnson conceded that Fortas was, of course, free to refuse to attend the conference, but if thousands of young men could sacrifice for their country in Vietnam, Fortas could do so by leaving private practice and taking the position on the Court. Fortas could hardly refuse. When Herblock, the famed *Washington Post* political cartoonist, turned his attention to the Fortas nomination, he chose to depict the new justice with his arm being twisted.[5]

The confirmation proceedings went like clockwork, a reminder

5. See Kalman, *Abe Fortas*, pp. 240–48. As Professor Kalman notes, this version of the nomination, recounted by both Fortas and Johnson, makes for a classic political tale. In reality, the appointment was not only expected but also welcomed, although Fortas did have some qualms about the timing.

of how confirmations had once worked. Lyndon Johnson's Great Society appeared to have revived the New Deal coalition, and, with liberalism the order of the day, neither Democrat nor Republican perceived any electoral gain from a serious challenge to the nominee. The activism of the Warren Court had not yet reached its zenith, and the impact of expanding the reach of judicial power was still unclear. The desegregation decisions notwithstanding, appointments to the Court, for all their importance, were not matters of political life and death to a host of powerful group interests. The Senate, though in the midst of change, still functioned in its post—World War II mode, and, when the leadership accepted Abe Fortas without objection, the nomination was, for all intents and purposes, a done deal. At the Judiciary Committee hearings Fortas minimized his relationship with LBJ (there were a few grumbles about the president's appointing one of his "cronies"), and when some witnesses contended that Fortas had been too sympathetic to communism in the 1930s, even the more conservative members of the committee rose in his defense.[6] A unanimous committee vote of approval came after less than three hours of hearings. Within two weeks of the formal nomination, the full Senate confirmed the new justice with a simple voice vote. From the perspective of the 1990s, a truly remarkable event had taken place: Abe Fortas, a friend of the president, a lifelong liberal and advocate of progressive politics, a champion of civil rights, a controversial defender of the weak and unpopular during the McCarthy era, had been confirmed justice of the Supreme Court without a single dissenting vote.

He would remain on the Court for a mere four years. During this brief tenure his was a consistent vote to safeguard the rights of the accused and to support the cause of the weak and downtrodden. In Fortas's view the judiciary was charged with the primary task of protecting individual rights, and he resolutely defended civil liberties. Justice Fortas, however, was not easily typecast as a "Warren Court liberal." He often, for instance, joined with the conservative members

6. See Shogan, *Question of Judgment*, pp. 113–17.

of the Court in defending business interests, narrowly interpreting the power of government to regulate and chiding his liberal colleagues for failing to appreciate the "real world" of business and finance. In short, Justice Fortas was in the unusual position of being at times the darling of both the American Civil Liberties Union and the *Wall Street Journal.*

After his rise to the high court, Fortas continued to serve the needs of two clients. One was Pablo Casals. Fortas had represented the famous cellist since the mid-1950s, negotiating among other things Casals's historic concert at the Kennedy White House. Casals was over ninety years of age when Fortas came to the Supreme Court, and Fortas made it quite clear that he was not inclined to attempt to explain to the aged musician that he could no longer act as his attorney.[7] His other client was the president of the United States. Lyndon Johnson simply could not do without his most trusted adviser, and as the Vietnam War and its political fallout ravaged both his domestic programs and his foreign policies, he continually sought Fortas's advice. Justice Fortas's involvement with the Johnson administration was far-reaching, ranging from active participation in the management of the Vietnam War to service as presidential speech writer. Although both Johnson and Fortas sought to hide this arrangement from public scrutiny, throughout the latter years of the Johnson presidency Washington was buzzing with rumors of the dual role played by Fortas. The rumors actually understated the reality; from the moment of his appointment to the Court, Fortas was an official member of the judicial branch and an unofficial, but terribly significant, member of the executive branch.[8]

In March of 1968 Johnson announced that he would not seek another term as president. The war in Vietnam and the war at home had destroyed his presidency. Two weeks before Johnson's announcement, Earl Warren celebrated his seventy-seventh birthday; though in

7. Ibid., p. 293.
8. The extent of Justice Fortas's connection with the Johnson administration is amply documented by his biographers. See ibid., chap. 14; Murphy, *Fortas*, chap. 10.

good health, he had spent over fifty years in the public service and now understandably might have anticipated retirement and leisure time away from the pressures of public life. But his decision to retire in the summer of 1968 was also the product of careful political calculation. Johnson's decision not to seek another term, combined with the general disarray of the Democratic party, virtually guaranteed a Republican victory in the fall. By announcing his retirement during the remaining months of the Johnson presidency, Warren believed he had made certain that LBJ, and not Richard Nixon, would name the new chief justice. The fact that Warren anticipated that Johnson would choose Abe Fortas for the post made the decision to retire that much easier.[9]

FORTAS ON TRIAL

A Few Whales and Many Minnows

No one understood the Senate quite as well as Lyndon Johnson did. In the brief span of his two terms in office, the senator from Texas had made a lasting mark on the institution, and his instinctive feel for the legislative process and the human side of the Senate became the stuff of legends.[10] The move to the vice-presidency and then to the White House did not diminish his legislative genius; Johnson's parliamentary skills, as well as the sheer force of his personality in one-on-one confrontations, were augmented by the aura of the presidency. During his years as president Johnson's mastery of the legislative process dazzled even his most jaded critics. The legislative record of the Johnson presidency was remarkable: the Civil Rights Act of 1964, the

9. G. Edward White, *Earl Warren: A Public Life* (New York: Oxford Univ. Press, 1982), pp. 306–13, describes Warren's thinking with respect to his retirement.

10. Senator J. William Fulbright: "When Lyndon was majority leader he was a master at managing the Senate and at reconciling people with diametrically opposed views. Nobody could match him. He knew every personal interest of every member of the Senate just like he knew the palm of his hand. He knew how to bring people together, because he could appeal to their different interests. If he asked Harry Byrd to do something, he always knew what it was that Harry wanted in return." Quoted in Merle Miller, *Lyndon: An Oral Biography* (New York: Putnam, 1980), p. 175.

Voting Rights Act of 1965, the Economic Opportunity Act, Medicare, comprehensive federal aid to education, and a host of redevelopment programs for economically ailing areas formed merely the tip of the Johnson legislative iceberg. The period of achievement was brief, but for several years in the mid-1960s Lyndon Johnson could lay claim to being the most effective president in modern American history. And no small measure of that success was owing to his understanding of the Senate.

Thus in June of 1968, when Johnson learned of Earl Warren's decision to retire as chief justice, he immediately plotted a strategy to elevate Abe Fortas to the post. In formulating a plan of action, Johnson relied on his extensive knowledge of the ways of the Senate. In his view, the Senate consisted of a few "whales" and many "minnows." The conventional wisdom held that in any battle in the Senate (particularly in securing its advice and consent on appointments), the president had to negotiate only with the appropriate whales. Once the consent of the powerful had been secured, the remainder of the Senate would fall into line. In the case of Fortas, there were two crucial whales. To guarantee success and to control sufficient votes to end a possible filibuster, Johnson felt he needed the support of either the Dixiecrats—the conservative bloc of southern Democrats who often balked at Johnson's Great Society legislative program—or several Republicans. He courted Richard Russell, the senior senator from Georgia, to secure the Dixiecrat vote. To balance the unpredictability of these southern Democrats, Johnson also sought Republican support from the minority leader, Everett Dirksen of Illinois.

During his years as majority leader, Johnson had often worked closely with Dirksen, and, when LBJ became president, Dirksen had provided needed Republican votes to break a southern filibuster and secure passage of the Civil Rights Act of 1964. Dirksen's aid never came cheap; for his backing of Fortas, Dirksen demanded continued support of the Subversive Activities Control Board.[11] When that deal

---

11. The SACB had been created in the early 1950s to identify Communists and Communist-controlled groups. The attorney general would bring cases before the SACB, and on the basis of these cases the SACB would publicize the list of supposed dangerous individuals and organizations. By the late 1960s the board was not only a vestige of the

was in place, Dirksen began his effort to provide a Republican cushion to the Fortas nomination. Several young Republican senators, led by freshman Robert Griffin of Michigan, had formed a group with the professed goal of blocking the nomination. Dirksen strove to undercut the upstarts, announcing that he would vote to break any filibuster and that a majority of Republicans was prepared to back Fortas. Because an insurgent group of young minnows was contrary to his understanding of the workings of the Senate, Johnson underestimated the potential of these Republicans to disrupt the orderly confirmation of Fortas. Nevertheless, the White House quietly responded by communicating with business interests in the states of the recalcitrant Republicans to put pressure on any senator considering bucking both the minority leader and the White House.[12] These efforts put the young Republicans on the defensive; the power of the executive to influence important constituents, plus statements by the Republican leadership that the insurgents were alone in opposing Fortas, set the minnows adrift in uncharted and dangerous waters. One of Dirksen's aides captured the prevailing mood: "Young guys just don't filibuster around here. If they are foolish enough to try it, they'll find that it doesn't work. And if, by some fluke, it should work, they'll pay for it."[13]

The courting of Russell was another matter. Russell had represented Georgia in the U.S. Senate since 1932. His seniority in the Senate made him the chair of the powerful Armed Services Committee and the de facto head of the Appropriations Committee. (The frail health of the chairman, Senator Hayden of Arizona, left Russell, the

---

McCarthy era but also a haven for political patronage. Dirksen, however, used his support of the SACB to solidify his standing among old-line conservatives and backed its continued funding. The Senate had agreed to fund the board only if the attorney general brought a case to the SACB by June 20, 1968 (no case had been brought in over two and one-half years). Ramsey Clark, the attorney general, believed the SACB a threat to civil liberties and was reluctant to give it continued life. Dirksen's payment in return for his support of Fortas was the president's promise to insist that the attorney general forward cases to the SACB. The story is detailed in Murphy, *Fortas,* pp. 294–97.

12. See Murphy, *Fortas,* pp. 316–17; Shogan, *Question of Judgment,* pp. 154–56.
13. Quoted in Murphy, *Fortas,* p. 325.

second-ranking Democrat on the committee, at the center of power.) Longtime service on the Democratic Steering Committee gave Russell an important voice in deciding the committee assignments of other Senate Democrats. Johnson's relationship with Russell stretched back to LBJ's early days in the Senate; recognizing legislative talent when he saw it, Russell had adopted the young Senator Johnson as his protégé, in effect commanding Senate Democrats in the early 1950s to make LBJ their leader. Russell's Senate "style" fit the institution perfectly; he was adept at compromise and displayed courtly manners and evident intelligence. No senator was more respected and none possessed greater power and influence, even though he did not hold a formal leadership position.

Russell was also the acknowledged leader of the southern Democratic delegation in the Senate. From the time he first came to the Senate, in 1933, through the mid-1960s, there were at least eleven votes to invoke cloture in connection with attempts to pass civil rights legislation.[14] Russell successfully led the battle against all of them and also fended off attempts to liberalize the cloture rule itself. When asked how the southern bloc of only eighteen senators could be so successful, Senator John Stennis of Mississippi replied that "we did not have eighteen Senators but that we have seventeen plus Senator Russell—and that plus Russell is the thing which makes the difference." Stennis paid Russell another dubious compliment. After Russell led the futile fight to block the Civil Rights Act of 1964, Stennis wrote him; "[E]xcept for you and your fine leadership, a strong civil rights bill would have been passed . . . as early as 1948 . . . or certainly after the unprecedented Supreme Court decision [*Brown* v. *Board of Education*] of 1954."[15] In the traditional understanding of the

14. Unlimited debate is perhaps the feature that most distinguishes the Senate from the House, and hence the filibuster is a jealously guarded Senate prerogative. It was not until 1917 that the Senate even adopted a cloture rule to end debate. Rule 22 of the Senate provided that debate be cut off if two-thirds of the senators present and voting agreed to a cloture motion. In 1975 the current cloture rule was enacted, requiring the vote of three-fifths of the Senate—sixty senators—to close debate.

15. Quoted in Gilbert C. Fite, *Richard Russell, Senator from Georgia* (Chapel Hill: Univ. of North Carolina Press, 1991), pp. 407, 416. While a testimony to Russell's

way the Senate operated, Russell could deliver votes. In short, he was the quintessential Senate whale.

Johnson thought that Russell's assent would clinch the Fortas nomination. To secure the Russell stamp of approval, Johnson nominated Texan Homer Thornberry, a judge on the Fifth Circuit Court of Appeals, to assume Fortas's associate justice seat. Thornberry was a competent jurist, not the equal of Fortas, but among the reasons for the selection of Thornberry was that he was an old duck-hunting buddy of Richard Russell. "When you sit in a duck blind all day with a man, you really get to know him," and Russell knew Thornberry "to be a good man, an able man and a fair man."[16] Johnson had no difficulty with the notion of putting Thornberry on the Court, and, if a Thornberry nomination would nail down Russell's vote on Fortas, then it would be done. Therefore it was scarcely a coincidence that Russell was having dinner with Johnson when the president called Thornberry to inform him of his nomination as associate justice. Russell promised Johnson that he would support the Fortas nomination and enthusiastically support Homer Thornberry. Johnson had secured the consent of the two critical whales in the Senate; his understanding of how the Senate worked led him to conclude that Abe Fortas would be the next chief justice.

The Crucible of the Senate Judiciary Committee

The hearings before the Senate Judiciary Committee on the nomination of Abe Fortas to be chief justice of the United States began on July 11, 1968. In the days immediately preceding the hearings, insid-

---

immense influence in the Senate, these statements also testify to Russell's unwavering defense of apartheid in America.

16. Quoted in Murphy, *Fortas*, p. 292. Clark Clifford argued against nominating Thornberry, urging Johnson to consider a moderate Republican for the associate justice spot. See Kalman, *Abe Fortas*, p. 328. With the aid of hindsight, Clifford was, of course, correct. A Republican in place of Thornberry might have done more to avoid Republican opposition than anything Dirksen could provide. In addition, by 1968 Russell's influence in the Senate and his ability to deliver the southern bloc had declined. See, for example, Fite, *Richard Russell*, chap. 20.

ers questioned whether the committee would request Fortas to appear personally and whether he would accept the invitation. Edward White and Harlan Fiske Stone, the two previous sitting justices nominated to become chief justice, had not personally testified before the committee. The questioning of a sitting justice raises a host of potential separation-of-powers difficulties, with both the nominee and the committee obligated to avoid discussion of past decisions and pending cases.[17] Nevertheless, the chairman of the Judiciary Committee, James Eastland, Democrat of Mississippi, was determined to have Fortas appear personally, and, although the White and Stone precedents offered a gracious and honorable way out, Fortas was outwardly confident of his ability to control the proceedings and win over the Senate and the public.[18]

As a rule, it is easier for an organized minority of senators to delay passage of a measure indefinitely in the U.S. Senate than for a loosely organized majority to secure prompt and decisive action. Delay is a particularly effective strategy in contesting a presidential nomination. Drawing the proceedings out over time permits the opposition to organize, new information to be discovered, the public to be aroused. In the case of the Fortas nomination, prolonging the hearings posed an additional threat to the nominee; the closer a final Senate vote to the November election, the more potent the argument

17. Technically Fortas was not the first sitting justice to testify before the Judiciary Committee. Recess appointments to the Court, made by the president while the Senate is not in session, permit the justice to be sworn in and engage in the Court's work although not formally confirmed by the Senate. When the Senate returns, the president renominates the individual to secure the advice and consent of the Senate. The "new" justice is then sworn in a second time. In the modern era, Earl Warren, William Brennan, and Potter Stewart received recess appointments and were subject to Senate proceedings while on the bench. Although Warren declined to appear before the committee, the Stewart hearings saw the nominee make a spirited defense of his commitment to the Court's efforts to desegregate southern school districts. No doubt because of the unseemliness of questioning sitting members of the Court, the Senate adopted a resolution in 1960 requesting the president to avoid recess appointments to the Court.

18. Behind the scenes, however, Fortas had misgivings. He even suggested that a Senate confirmation of a sitting justice as chief justice was unnecessary and urged friends to push that position on friendly members of the Judiciary Committee. See Kalman, *Abe Fortas*, p. 335.

to save the nomination of the new chief justice for the incoming president. With the Senate scheduled to recess in August, extended hearings would allow Fortas's opponents to delay a committee vote until September. The first day of the hearings therefore set the initial tone, producing a listless debate over whether there indeed was a vacancy on the Court. The Warren retirement letter had not set a specific date for his departure; he had retired effective at the pleasure of the president, and Johnson in turn accepted "at such time as a successor is qualified." In the view of several of Fortas's opponents on the committee, this conditional resignation meant, in effect, there was no current vacancy on the Court. The debate proved inconsequential, but it consumed a full day of the committee's time. The testimony of Fortas was further delayed when Senator Sam Ervin, Democrat of North Carolina, requested additional time to study all of Fortas's written opinions. It was not until July 16 that the star witness took his place before the committee.

The White House had hoped Fortas could complete his testimony in one day; it would take four. Although wide-ranging, the inquiry was anchored by two general areas of concern. The first was the justice's connections with Lyndon Johnson. When nominated to the Court in 1965, he had been quizzed about his role as adviser to the president, but, as a private citizen, Fortas had been free to serve the president in any mutually agreeable capacity. Now, however, he was a Supreme Court justice and governed by the doctrine of separation of powers. Grilled by the members of the committee regarding his role in the Johnson administration, Fortas, at best, was less than forthright and, at worst, simply lied. He skillfully avoided admitting outright impropriety, but the tone of his testimony cast a pall over the hearings and troubled even his most ardent supporters and friends.

More troublesome, still, was the effort of several members of the committee to make the Fortas nomination a national referendum on the ideological direction of the Warren Court. Since the 1954 decision in *Brown* v. *Board of Education*, conservative and southern hostility to the Warren Court had grown, stimulated by the Court's continuing commitment to racial integration and its efforts to extend the application of the procedural safeguards found in the Bill of Rights to state criminal proceedings. The Court's criminal process decisions provided several of Fortas's opponents on the committee with their best material. With the explosion in crime and judicial restrictions on police behavior soon to be themes of the Republican drive to the presidency, emphasizing the often gruesome details of these decisions in queries to the nominee appeared to be a no-lose proposition. Fortas might refuse to respond, on the basis of the impropriety of discussing actual cases, and risk appearing evasive, or he could attempt the tasks almost impossible in a public forum, of providing technical, legal explanations for what would soon be notorious decisions. In either case, the nominee would make an unfavorable impression, and the strategy quickly developed to place the burden of fifteen years of Supreme Court decision making directly on the shoulders of one man.

His principal antagonist was Senator Strom Thurmond.[19] For hours Thurmond berated Fortas for many of the Warren Court's criminal process decisions, and Fortas, choosing to refrain from discussing these decisions, remained silent. Thurmond then turned the inquiry to *Mallory* v. *United States,* a 1957 decision in which the Court reversed the conviction of a confessed rapist because the police had failed in a timely manner to bring the defendant before a magistrate as required by federal law.[20] "There was really no question that he committed the crime," Thurmond thundered,

19. As governor of South Carolina, Thurmond had bolted the Democratic party in 1948, running for president on the States' Rights ticket. He returned to the Democratic party, only to support Barry Goldwater in 1964 and change party affiliation, becoming one of the leaders of the Republican resurgence in the South. Representing South Carolina in the Senate since 1954, Thurmond was an avid defender of the "southern way of life" and established the modern Senate record for individual filibuster, speaking on the floor of the Senate for twenty-four hours and eighteen minutes in a personal campaign to prevent passage of the 1957 voting rights bill.

20. 354 U.S. 449. Mallory, a nineteen-year-old black man, had been arrested in Washington, D.C., and charged with rape. Police interrogated him for seven hours prior to arraignment and secured a confession. Mallory eventually appealed to the Supreme Court, and the Court, in a unanimous decision, reversed the conviction because the police had intentionally delayed bringing him before a magistrate for arraignment—in direct violation of federal rules of criminal procedure—to obtain a confession. After his release, Mallory was arrested and convicted of assault in Philadelphia.

but when it went to the Supreme Court, they reversed the case and the man went free. Why did he go free? A criminal, a convict, a guilty man, who committed a serious rape on a lady in this city. Simply because the Court said they held him a little too long before arraignment. Do you believe in that kind of justice? Don't you think the main purpose of the courthouses, of the judges, of the jury is to go to the heart of the case and render justice, to convict them when they are guilty, and turn them loose when they are free, and not let technicalities control the outcome? And isn't that what happened in this case?

When Fortas demurred, refusing to respond to inquiries about particular decisions, Thurmond exploded,

Does not that decision, Mallory, I want that word to ring in your ears—Mallory—the man happened to have been from my state incidentally—shackle law enforcement? Mallory, a man who raped a woman, admitted his guilt and the Supreme Court turned him loose on a technicality. And who I was told later went to Philadelphia and committed another crime, and somewhere else another crime, because the court turned him loose on technicalities. Is not that type of decision calculated to bring the courts and the law and the administration in disrepute? Is not that type of decision calculated to encourage some people to commit rapes and serious crimes? Can you as a Justice of the Supreme Court condone such a decision? I ask you to answer that question.[21]

Stunned by the intensity of this outburst, Fortas could do little except decline to discuss the merits of the decision. Regaining his composure, Thurmond continued, in case after case, to demand explanations for a host of Supreme Court decisions that appeared, at least in his view, to turn on mere technicalities and, taken together, to result in a crisis of law and order. It was a theme repeated almost daily in the ensuing presidential campaign. Although Thurmond's outburst

21. The Fortas-Thurmond exchange took place during the July 19, 1968, session of the Fortas-Thornberry hearings.

may have shocked some observers, his making Fortas the scapegoat for the sins of the Warren Court (*Mallory* had been decided a full seven years before Fortas assumed his seat on the Court) was an effective strategy. Moreover, it took up precious time. When an exhausted Fortas concluded his testimony, the committee had yet to hear from several other witnesses, and the agony of Abe Fortas continued.

One of these witnesses was James Clancy, an attorney representing Citizens for a Decent Literature. Outraged by an alleged increase in pornography throughout the land, Clancy's group had purportedly analyzed Supreme Court obscenity decisions, concluding that in some forty-nine cases Fortas had provided the critical vote permitting a majority of the Court to hold the material in question to be not obscene. To illustrate the depth of this continuing depravity, Clancy had produced a slide show highlighting some of the material involved in these cases, as well as one of the films the Court had held to be constitutionally protected. He invited the members of the committee and other senators to view the evidence, and the committee leadership gratefully accepted, adjourning the hearings and ordering the full committee to delay its report for another week to allow senators to consider Clancy's material. For the next several days, a projector was set up in a room in the Capitol, and senators were invited to view X-rated movies. Not only did this delay the proceedings—by now it was clear the Senate would not vote until after the August recess—but an appearance in the viewing room provided senators with a convenient rationale for opposing the nomination. A conscientious senator, after viewing *Flaming Creatures* (a full-length feature added to the Senate collection after the Clancy testimony), was hardly expected to announce that the experience fortified his support for the embattled Fortas.

In mid-September the Judiciary Committee voted, 11 to 6, to report favorably on the nomination. Liberals formed a majority on the committee, and the favorable vote was not unexpected, but neither was the filibuster that began when the nomination reached the Senate floor. When a cloture vote failed by a substantial margin, the Fortas nomination was dead. Fortas requested Johnson to withdraw his name from consideration, and a little over a week later the president announced he would make no further nominations to the Court. Earl Warren would remain chief justice, his replacement to be named by the new president.[22]

ABE FORTAS AND THE NEW POLITICS OF JUDICIAL CONFIRMATIONS

The Old World Is Rapidly Changing

The Fortas nomination was undone by events and political considerations that made Fortas the wrong candidate for the wrong position at the wrong time. The fact that Lyndon Johnson was a lame-duck president undercut his celebrated control of the legislative process. Charges of cronyism and Justice Fortas's close connections with the administration raised conflict-of-interest and separation-of-powers problems that transcended simple partisan politics. Conservative outrage at the Warren Court was a major factor. With the wisdom provided by a quarter century of hindsight, however, one must conclude that the Fortas nomination fell victim to circumstances far beyond the power of either Lyndon Johnson or Abe Fortas to control. Although both men had often exhibited an extraordinary ability to shape their own destiny, by 1968 these masters of the old political

22. The tragedy of Abe Fortas continued. Following the failed nomination to the chief justiceship, Fortas returned to the Court as associate justice. In May of 1969 *Life* magazine released a story detailing Fortas's connection with Louis Wolfson, a man found guilty of conspiracy to violate the federal securities laws. The story is a complicated one, detailed in the Murphy and the Kalman biographies of Fortas. To make a long story quite short, Fortas had represented Wolfson during his years in private practice. Wolfson had established a philanthropic foundation, and when Fortas came to the Supreme Court, Wolfson offered him the position of consultant to the foundation at a stipend of $20,000 a year for life. Fortas accepted the first payment but then reconsidered the arrangement, resigned from the position, and returned the money several months later. The gist of the *Life* story was entirely accurate: a Supreme Court justice had taken money from a foundation headed by a man subsequently found to have violated the federal securities law. Shortly after publication of the story, Justice Fortas resigned from the Court.

order had been blindsided by sweeping changes that altered the basic structure of American politics and institutions.

It is indeed remarkable that Lyndon Johnson could have been so wrong about the Senate he knew so well. He had cultivated the principal whales, and yet neither Richard Russell nor Everett Dirksen ultimately delivered. Both men had convenient explanations for their defections, but behind the rhetoric was the reality that neither could control and deliver votes as they had in the past.[23] For his part, Johnson, educated in the structured ways of the old Senate, simply could not imagine that a band of renegade young Republican senators would consider defying Everett Dirksen or that Richard Russell was no longer the behind-the-scenes master of the Senate. Evolution in the Senate had taken a strange twist—the whales had fallen victim to the minnows—and one of the primary casualties of the new arrangement was Abe Fortas. In less than a decade following the defeat of Fortas, it would be clear to all that the Senate whale was an extinct species.

The Senate as Johnson knew it was an institution whose membership was constrained by sharply defined and well-understood norms of behavior that rewarded conformity and specialization, demanded that newcomers serve a substantial apprenticeship, and discouraged the maverick. By the last years of his presidency, this model of Senate behavior was out of step with the more open, visible, media-oriented politics of modern America. Indeed, one might easily conclude that the failed Fortas nomination was one of the first important indicators of the transformation of the Senate into a more open institution that provides individual members with the resources and motivation to champion diverse interests without regard to state

23. The ostensible reason for Russell is reneging on his word to support Fortas was the administration's delay in clearing a federal district court judgeship for one of Russell's friends and supporters. Although the nomination was eventually cleared by the administration, the delay, in the view of Russell, made it appear that he had struck a deal in which he voted for Fortas in return for the district court judgeship. The appearance of such crass political patronage, Russell concluded, released him from any obligation to support Fortas. Dirksen announced right before the cloture vote that the committee hearings on Fortas raised new issues, which demanded greater scrutiny, and hence he was now neutral with regard to the nomination. See Murphy, *Fortas*, chap. 14 and pp. 521–22.

boundaries, seniority, or issue specialization. Today the Senate as an institution is far less hierarchical and stable than it was when Lyndon Johnson was majority leader, and one consequence of this is to make the politics of judicial confirmations highly volatile and quite unpredictable.

The animosity the Warren Court triggered among conservative senators was, perhaps, the heaviest burden. Linking Fortas to controversial Supreme Court decisions was an astute political strategy, and southern senators like Strom Thurmond played their parts perfectly. Quite apart from strategy and political grandstanding, however, the battle over the Fortas nomination did reveal many senators' deep antagonism to the direction of modern constitutional law. In their opinion the Supreme Court under Earl Warren had provoked explosive change that threatened the stability of their political and social world. They were indeed angry, and, from the perspective of the defenders of the status quo, their anger was quite justified. The Warren Court did bring about a judicial revolution, although the Court's obscenity decisions were a small and insignificant part of that revolution.

Throughout the 1960s the Warren Court reconceived the nature of judicial power by opening the doors of the federal courthouse to a host of new litigants and providing successful litigants with an expanded array of judicial remedies. As will be explained in chapter 2, the Court redefined modern judicial liberalism, rejecting the New Deal model of judicial modesty and restraint for a defiant activism designed to benefit America's disadvantaged. This break with the jurisprudence of the New Deal was the Court's most revolutionary act, because augmenting the ability of the federal judiciary to serve the needs of group litigants ultimately benefited not simply the poor and disenfranchised but many middle- and upper-middle-class interests that found the judiciary a useful arena in which to realize policy goals. Thus a quite unintended consequence of the Warren Court revolution was to make the nomination and confirmation of federal judges a high-stakes political event with broad policy implications. Not the least of Johnson's miscalculations during the Fortas affair was his failure to appreciate that an appointment to the Supreme Court had become too important to too many potent political forces for insider deals between the president and a few Senate whales to go unchallenged.

Amplifying the impact of these developments was the fact that in 1968 the latent fault lines in the New Deal coalition split wide open. A by-product of the hegemony of the Democratic party in the years following the New Deal was the diminished significance of judicial appointments; during this period there was little incentive for forces in the Democratic party to break ranks and challenge the governing consensus on the appointment of judges. Even the years of the Eisenhower presidency did little to change this understanding of the confirmation process; the appointment of federal judges remained a low-key affair, with senators typically unwilling or unable to invest substantial political capital in any attempt to challenge judicial nominations. When the governing coalition fell upon hard times, however, even the politics of judicial appointments began to reflect the deep divisions within the party. By 1968, for example, the typical southern Senate Democrat saw little political gain in supporting Fortas and little political cost in challenging his own party's presidential prerogative.

The Republican party was also in a period of transition, and, in his campaign to forge a new Republican majority, Richard Nixon attacked the Supreme Court in a manner calculated to attract disaffected white Democrats to his party. The image of a federal judiciary protecting the forces of disorder and discontent at the expense of law-abiding citizens became a powerful campaign theme in the resurgence of the national Republican party. Throughout the 1970s and 1980s the Court remained a valuable bogeyman for many Republican candidates, providing a convenient explanation for the party's inability to enact the social agenda championed by its most conservative elements. Although in 1968 veteran Senate whales like Everett Dirksen might consider nominations to the Court appropriate for behind-the-scenes deals, a new generation of Senate Republicans understood that highly visible, public battles to bring the Court back to the "silent majority" could produce real electoral dividends that would outweigh the consequences of any breach of timeworn patterns of Senate decorum and behavior.

Back to the Future

The events surrounding the failed Fortas nomination thus provide a benchmark for the study of the new politics of judicial selection and confirmation. With very few exceptions, previous judicial confirmations in the twentieth century were characterized by low-key, insider politics in which a handful of participants made the critical decisions with minimal public scrutiny or participation. Following the Fortas nomination came the modern era of conflict in which open, public confrontations over the selection of our judges made confirmation to the Court a highly unpredictable enterprise. Fortas links these two eras, providing a window on both the past and the present. And the tale of Abe Fortas, despite its seductive combination of triumph and tragedy, human virtue and foible, does compel the observer seeking a greater understanding of contemporary American politics to eschew, at least for a moment, the fascination with the particular and to direct attention to several recent changes in American politics and law that have combined to alter the general political landscape.

Chapter 2

THE JUDICIARY: THE CHANGING NATURE OF JUDICIAL POWER

From 1962 through Earl Warren's retirement, in 1969, the Supreme Court altered the nature of judicial power in the United States. Since the days of John Marshall, the political effectiveness of the federal judiciary has hinged on the ability of astute judges to use the great power of judicial review to link the judiciary to influential social and political forces. This basic tenet of judicial power historically aligned the Court with the forces of capital; for almost 150 years constitutional interpretation offered an effective method of defending property against the regulatory power of the state. Efforts at reform in the United States therefore often included attempts to weaken the Court or, at the very least, to constrict the scope of judicial review. To the generation of reformers associated with the New Deal, for example, breaking the link between the judiciary and capital became the touchstone of successful liberal reform.

In seeking to sever the bond between the judiciary and industrial capitalism, the progressive jurists of the first half of the twentieth century endeavored to interpret narrowly rules governing the timing of and parties to federal lawsuits as well as the nature of issues federal courts might properly decide. The "real" Warren Court revolution, which assumes a prominent role in the analysis that follows, directly challenged the New Deal liberal's faith in a diminished judicial role as a condition for reform. In their fervor to empower the politically disadvantaged, the justices of the Warren Court redefined modern judicial liberalism, easing the requirements for the entertaining of federal lawsuits and providing an expanding range of litigants with an array of new judicial remedies. With the doors of the federal

*courthouses thrown wide open, a multitude of groups—including many
affluent, upper-middle-class interests—rushed in to find the judiciary a
useful ally in the battle to secure their political goals.*

*There is, then, a direct connection between the judicial activism of the
modern Supreme Court and the politics of the modern confirmation process.
In the last thirty years many politically potent groups have come to consider
the staffing of the Supreme Court and the lower federal courts to be of
striking importance and the effort to influence the selection process worth the
expenditure of substantial resources. To place the impact of judicial activism
on the confirmation process in context, however, we must begin at some
distance. The first step is to sketch briefly the growing significance of the idea
of judicial restraint to the reform movements of the early twentieth century
in order to put in perspective the "real" revolution of the Warren Court and
its impact on the modern process of selecting and confirming the justices of
the Supreme Court.*

THE CRISIS OF THE OLD ORDER

Judicial Activism in Defense of Property

Political power in the United States is inevitably a function of constituency. In a nation with a strong commitment to popular rule, mass
support is often the crucial component in the struggle for political
supremacy. Institutions typically grow more politically dominant as
they come to represent the interests of larger portions of the electorate. Political actors that lack a direct link to a sizable constituency play
a secondary role. During much of the twentieth century, for example,
the executive branch has dominated political life principally because
the presidency has proven best suited to using modern technology to
reach out to a nationwide constituency. Recent congressional challenges to the power of the modern presidency, on the other hand,
highlight the heightened capacity of individual senators to attract
national attention through the skillful use of the media and to extend
their popular support beyond state borders.

The framers also understood well the significance of constituency; the judiciary was thought to be "the least dangerous branch" precisely because of the limited capability of the courts to cultivate and mobilize mass support. Article III of the Constitution, for example, grants federal judges lifetime tenure, a unique bequest of political independence. But autonomy is not necessarily synonymous with political power. Elected officials in the United States may periodically face the harrowing prospect of defeat at the polls, but victory provides a measure of democratic legitimacy unavailable to appointed judges. The framers were confident that the judicial branch lacked both the political validity conferred by popular sovereignty and the institutional resources to develop strong and lasting bonds to important constituent groups. In the grand design of the Constitution, they believed, the judiciary would play a secondary role in the development of the American state.

Had the Supreme Court been content with its initial, peripheral position, the selection of justices would be of little consequence even today. Establishing the Court as a primary, national political institution, however, called for a judiciary able to forge alliances with important political and economic forces.[1] John Marshall's famous opinion in *Marbury* v. *Madison* was a critical first step because in announcing the power of judicial review—the power of the federal judiciary to declare the acts of other branches null and void as contrary to the Constitution—Marshall established the Court as the final arbiter of the meaning of the Constitution and thereby made the judiciary an attractive institutional ally for powerful groups.[2] Max Lerner astutely noted that the genius of Marshall was in forging "the strategic link between capitalism and constitutionalism."[3] During Marshall's thirty-four years as chief justice, the Court emerged as the

1. See Mark Silverstein and Benjamin Ginsberg, "The Supreme Court and the New Politics of Judicial Power," *Political Science Quarterly* 102 (1987): 371, for a discussion of the links between federal judiciary power and constituency support.

2. *Marbury* v. *Madison*, 1 Cranch 137 (1803).

3. Max Lerner, "John Marshall and the Campaign of History," in Leonard Levy, ed., *American Constitutional Law: Historical Essays* (New York: Harper & Row, 1966), p. 57.

prime protector of private property against democratically elected state legislatures thought to be too sympathetic to the leveling impulses of the propertyless masses. By joining the judiciary's role of interpreting the Constitution with the political power of the prosperous, the Marshall Court was able to transcend the institutional constraints on judicial power.

Marshall's legacy (he died in 1835) to future generations of American judges was to establish the potential for active judicial intervention in the affairs of state. Less skillful jurists or those less favored by historical circumstance would still find the assertion of judicial power a risky endeavor. Marshall's successor, Roger Taney, shared his vision of an activist judiciary, but the social and economic life of America had become vastly more complicated by midcentury and the exercise of judicial power a more intricate undertaking. The Court was forced to temper its defense of property in the face of growing popular support for state regulatory activity that impaired private economic rights in the cause of expanding economic opportunity for the community at large. Reconciling the tension between the conservative insistence on stable, predictable laws governing economic relations, on the one hand, and the progressive quest for more flexible constitutional interpretation to release creative economic energy, on the other, proved a formidable challenge to the judges of the post-Marshall era.[4] The rising tide of states' rights sentiments and the explosive issue of slavery left the Taney Court unable to fashion enduring bonds with powerful social and economic forces. The Court's attempt to settle these issues in the infamous *Dred Scott* was a political and legal disaster.[5] Abandoned by its supporters and

4. The best example of this tension appears in the famous case of *Charles River Bridge* v. *Warren Bridge*, 36 U.S. 420 (1837), and the debate in that case between Chief Justice Taney and Justice Story over the relationship between the state and private property rights in a capitalist society remains a classic. See Stanley I. Kutler, *Privilege and Creative Destruction: The Charles River Bridge Case* (New York: Norton, 1978).

5. *Dred Scott* v. *Sandford*, 60 U.S. 393 (1857). Taney's opinion, perhaps the most disastrous one the Supreme Court has ever issued, held that blacks were not citizens under the meaning of the Constitution and that the Missouri Compromise Act, prohibiting slavery in the territories of the United States, was unconstitutional. The decision provoked outrage in the North and subjected the Court to a blizzard of abuse.

stripped of the prestige it had so carefully cultivated, the Court entered a period of decline and quiescence.

The Civil War stands as the critical divide in American political and economic history. The grand debates over the very nature of the Union that dominated the Marshall and Taney eras of Court history were ultimately settled not in the courtroom but on the battlefield. The nation that began as an agrarian society, where most citizens scratched out a living from the land, witnessed in the war's aftermath a great migration to the cities and the coming of the Industrial Revolution. A period of unprecedented economic development followed, producing extremes of wealth and poverty unsurpassed in America's history. At the turn of the century, it was reported that Marshall Field, the Chicago department store magnate, was clearing approximately $600 an hour from the operation of his store while paying the average clerk $12 for a sixty-hour workweek. The Census Bureau estimated that 9 percent of the nation's families owned 71 percent of the nation's wealth. As the transformation of America's economic life proceeded at a dizzying pace, the triumph of capital was aided by a sympathetic Supreme Court that found in the Constitution stringent limits on the power of government to regulate private enterprise. An expansive interpretation of the due process clause of the Fourteenth Amendment and a narrow construction of the powers of the national government made the Supreme Court the darling of the new industrial capitalists of the Gilded Age. Armed with the support of this powerful political ally, the Court could again return to center stage.

The Age of Reform

In the last quarter of the nineteenth century, the Supreme Court championed the cause of entrepreneurial liberty through a series of decisions that limited the reach of governmental power and directly linked the Court with the new forces of industrial and finance capitalism.[6] The ascendancy of this new industrial order ignited a deter-

6. For a highly readable account of the Court's interpretation of constitutional protections of property, see James W. Ely, *The Guardian of Every Other Right: A Constitu-*

mined opposition, and, beginning with the agrarian uprisings of the 1890s, the demand for a more effective use of state and federal governments to control the reach and abuses of private power provided an attractive alternative to the dogma of free markets and laissez-faire capitalism. Progressive of this era, however, could hardly be described as Jeffersonian romantics, animated by a faith in the wisdom of the populace and the dream of the return to an idyllic, agrarian America. Accepting industrialization and economic inequality as facts of modern life, they sought in big government administered by trained, disinterested experts the means to control and regulate capitalist development to further the public good. "The democrat," wrote Walter Lippmann in 1922, "has always assumed if political power can be derived in the right way, it would be beneficent." This naïveté was "the democratic fallacy." In the initial decades of the twentieth century, Progressives like Lippmann lived by the credo that "what determines the quality of civilization is the use made of power."[7]

The major obstacle to the effective use of governmental power to further the public good was the Supreme Court. From the very outset of the twentieth century, judicial activism on behalf of industrial capitalism and government regulation in the name of economic and social welfare were on a collision course. As the Progressive reformer increasingly looked to the state to control the expanding private sector, the industrial capitalist looked to a sympathetic Supreme Court to use the power of judicial review and constitutional interpretation to shield private power from state control. While the National Association of Manufacturers was passing resolutions praising the Supreme Court for its defense of economic liberty, the champions of reform were pressing a campaign to limit the scope of judicial review, on the basis of a growing conviction that an activist judiciary was the enemy of progressive reform.

---

tional History of Property Rights (New York: Oxford Univ. Press, 1992), particularly chap. 5, detailing the Court's decisions during the Gilded Age.

    7. Walter Lippmann, *Public Opinion* (New York: Free Press, 1965; original copyright 1922), p. 196. The classic work that inspired many of the Progressive reformers of the era was Herbert Croly's *The Promise of American Life* (1909).

Renovating a constitutional jurisprudence keyed to the protection of private property in light of the demands of modern industrial life became the intellectual passion of many of America's best and brightest during the initial decades of the twentieth century. The early career of Felix Frankfurter provides a prime example. Years before his appointment to the Supreme Court, Professor Frankfurter of the Harvard Law School was a respected advocate of progressive politics. Joining a defense of a powerful state run by impartial, expert administrators with expressions of grave misgivings concerning the exercise of judicial power, Frankfurter often employed the pages of the popular press to champion judicial restraint as an important step toward progressive reform. Repeatedly he sought to disabuse the populace of "the mischievous assumption that our judges embody pure reason, that they are set apart from the concerns of the community, regardless of time, place and circumstances, to become the interpreters of self-determining words with fixed content, yielding their meaning to a process of inexorable reasoning."[8] The exercise of constitutional adjudication and interpretation was, at bottom, a political event, and in matters of politics the judiciary had consciously to defer to the reasonable judgments of the other branches of government. Diminishing the role of the federal judiciary, he believed, was necessary to allow democratic government to respond to the needs of a modern industrial society. Active judicial intervention in the affairs of state was incompatible with progressive politics. Even when judicial activism produced the occasional liberal result, Frankfurter counseled caution. "For ourselves," he wrote after one such decision, "we regard the cost of this power of the Supreme Court on the whole as greater than its gains."[9]

---

8. "The Nomination of Mr. Justice Brandeis," *New Republic*, Feb. 5, 1916. Although unsigned, this editorial piece was written by Frankfurter. See Philip Kurland, ed., *Felix Frankfurter on the Supreme Court* (Cambridge: Harvard Univ. Press, 1970), p. 43, where the piece is reprinted.

9. "Can the Supreme Court Guarantee Toleration?" *New Republic*, June 17, 1925, reprinted in Kurland, *Felix Frankfurter*, p. 176. This piece was written in response to the decision in *Pierce* v. *Society of Sisters*, 268 U.S. 510 (1925), in which the Court used an expansive interpretation of due process to strike down an Oregon law that would have abolished private schools.

The judiciary's determined defense of industry led some reformers a step further, to support congressional proposals, ranging from
requiring a specified number of justices to agree before a federal law
might be declared unconstitutional to requiring the direct election of
federal judges for ten-year terms, all designed to restrict the ability of
the federal judiciary to declare legislative acts unconstitutional. The
measures prompted vigorous debate in Congress, scholarly journals,
and the popular press. Although none of the measures were ever
enacted, the idea of formally restricting the power of judicial review
was not without popular support. Even Frankfurter succumbed to the
reformer's frustration with hyperactive judicial review. So great was
his disaffection with the Supreme Court's use of the Fourteenth
Amendment to strike down innovative state legislation that in 1922
he announced in the pages of the *New Republic* his support of the
drastic step of repealing that amendment's due process clause.[10]

THE NEW DEAL AND A NEW JUDICIAL LIBERALISM

Holmes and Brandeis

Frankfurter eventually moderated his views, concluding that "pana-
ceas like the recall of judicial decisions or the requirement that more
than a majority of the Court should declare legislation unconstitutional" were not the answers.[11] Eschewing direct limitations on judicial power, Frankfurter, with a host of liberals in the years prior to the
New Deal, championed a jurisprudence of self-restraint that demanded that judges proceed in a statesmanlike manner, moderating

10. "An informed study of the work of the Supreme Court of the United States will
probably lead to the conclusion that no nine men are wise enough and good enough to
be entrusted with the power the unlimited provisions of the due process clauses confer.
We have had fifty years of experiment with the Fourteenth Amendment and the centralizing authority lodged with the Supreme Court over the domestic affairs of forty-eight
widely different States is an authority which it simply cannot discharge with safety to
either itself or the States. The due process clause ought to go." "The Red Terror of Judicial
Reform," *New Republic*, Oct. 1, 1924, unsigned editorial, see Kurland, *Felix Frankfurter*, pp.
166–67.
    11. Ibid., p. 226.

the impact of judicial review through a real deference to the decisions of the elected branches of government. In the years that followed, the doctrine of judicial self-restraint became the centerpiece of a new understanding of judicial liberalism and the hallmark of the jurisprudence of the New Deal.

The role model for this generation of liberals was Justice Oliver Wendell Holmes. The judges of the old order measured social legislation against fixed, immutable principles such as that of liberty of contract without apparent regard for new economic and social conditions. Progressives, on the other hand, believed that modern civilization was in a state of constant flux and required governments capable of adapting policies to the shifting needs of a dynamic society. From their perspective a judiciary that found in the Constitution a set of unchanging first principles that severely circumscribed legislative attempts to grapple with the social ills of a changing society was anathema. The appeal of Holmes to liberals like John Dewey lay in his refusal to settle "matters of social policy by dialectic reasoning from fixed concepts."[12] For Holmes the core principle of majority rule defined the judicial role; unless the actions of the sovereign majority were entirely unreasonable, the task of the modern judge was to defer to the legislative choice, whatever the apparent wisdom of the challenged legislation.[13]

Holmes's jurisprudence of restraint freed the governing process from judicial control and placed ultimate responsibility for governing in the hands of the elected branches. Although a friend and mentor to many of the most influential liberals of the times and beloved by millions of Americans, Holmes had little faith in legislative efforts to

12. John Dewey, "Justice Holmes and the Liberal Mind," *New Republic*, Jan. 11, 1928, p. 210.
13. An often recounted story about Holmes illustrates the point. Encountering John W. Davis, the solicitor general, after he had argued an antitrust case before the Court, Holmes asked if there were many additional antitrust cases the solicitor general intended to bring to the Court. When Davis answered quite a few, Holmes responded, "Well bring 'em on and we'll decide 'em. Of course I know and every sensible man knows that the Sherman law is damned nonsense but if my country wants to go to hell, I'm here to help it." Quoted in Mark Silverstein, *Constitutional Faiths: Felix Frankfurter, Hugo Black and the Process of Judicial Decision Making* (Ithaca: Cornell Univ. Press, 1984), p. 44.

aid the poor and weak; in his world view the strong and powerful would inevitably win out and social welfare legislation designed to alter this outcome was doomed to failure. Despite his own fatalistic outlook Holmes became the archetype of the ideal judge to a generation of reformers because his understanding of the judicial role diminished the scope of judicial control while expanding that of the legislative and executive branches, and this fit neatly with the goals of those championing change and reform.

Liberals might differ over the means to achieve their goals, but in the years preceding the New Deal almost all agreed on the necessity of decreasing the sphere of judicial decision making as an important step in permitting the elected branches the flexibility to deal effectively with issues of the day. Justice Louis Brandeis, for example, unquestionably lacked Holmes's skepticism but joined in his colleague's efforts to moderate judicial authority over economic and social legislation. Acutely aware of the Supreme Court's tenuous claim to democratic legitimacy, Brandeis constantly reminded his brethren on the bench that "the most important thing we do is not doing" and strove to develop judicially enforced rules to carry out the ideal of restraint. His efforts in a case arising out of congressional attempts to control child labor illustrate this point.

During his career as a private attorney, Brandeis had been an outspoken leader in the progressive movement and a tireless campaigner to end the social and economic inequities of American life, including the evils of child labor. On the Court he often joined with Holmes to protest the conservative majority's zeal in protecting private property against legislative efforts to combat the social ills of a modern industrial society. In 1918, for example, he joined Holmes's famous dissent in *Hammer* v. *Dagenhart*, protesting the majority's holding that Congress lacked power under the commerce clause to exclude goods produced by child labor from interstate commerce.[14] Following the setback of *Hammer*, Congress attempted to limit child labor by imposing a substantial tax on any goods

14. 247 U.S. 251 (1918).

produced by children under the age of sixteen.[15] In *Atherton Mills* v. *Johnston,* the father of a young boy employed at Atherton Mills brought an action against the company alleging that because of the Child Labor Tax Act the company was about to discharge his son.[16] He sought a declaration that the act was unconstitutional and injunctive relief preventing the company from firing the boy. Atherton Mills acknowledged the proposed termination, but defended it on the basis that it was simply conforming to the federal act. A federal district court held the tax invalid and granted the requested relief.

Even though he was a constant critic of the evils of child labor and no doubt believed that the federal government had the constitutional authority to outlaw the practice, Brandeis wrote a memo to his fellow justices urging that the case be dismissed, for lack of jurisdiction, without their deciding the merits of the constitutional claim. An employer under the existing law, he noted, was free to discharge an employee at will, and as a result the father and the son had no cause of action against the company. Their dispute was with the government of the United States, which was not a party to the case. This defect could not be cured simply by amending the complaint to include the government as defendant, because a congressional act foreclosed any actions against the United States to restrain the collection of a tax. In this context, the constitutionality of the act could be tested only by the employer's first paying the tax and then raising the constitutional claim in an action against the government for a refund. Concluding that *Atherton* failed to present a "case" within the meaning of Article III of the Constitution, Brandeis urged the Court not to rush to judgment on the merits but simply to dismiss the action. He closed his memo as follows:

> For nearly a century and a quarter Federal courts, as an incident to deciding cases rightfully before them, have necessarily

15. This act was eventually struck down in *Bailey* v. *Drexel Furniture Co.,* 259 U.S. 20 (1922).

16. 259 U.S. 13 (1922).

exercised at times the solemn duty of declaring acts of Congress void. But the long continued, uninterrupted exercise of this power has not sufficed to silence the doubt originally expressed whether the framers of the Constitution intended to confer it. On the contrary, the popular protest against its exercise has never been as vehement, nor has it ever secured the support of so many political thinkers and writers, as in the last decade. At a time like the present, when the fundamental principles upon which our institutions rest are being seriously questioned, those who have faith in their wisdom and desire to preserve them unimpaired, can best uphold the Constitution by careful observance of the limitations which it imposes. As this court declared in the *Sinking Fund Cases*, "One branch of the Government cannot encroach upon the domain of another without danger. The safety of our institutions depends in no small degree on a strict observance of this salutary rule."[17]

The "careful observance of the limitations" on judicial decision making quickly became an article of faith for liberals of the day. They believed that the rigid observance of the rules of justiciability—the technical term used to describe the constitutional as well as the self-imposed, prudential limits on judicial power—would best preserve the separation of powers and ensure that the federal courts did not gratuitously exercise the power of judicial review. By confining the sphere of judicial influence through essentially discretionary rules, the judiciary could avoid more draconian limitations while allowing a powerful president and executive branch the constitutional "space" to provide the flexible leadership necessary in a modern industrial state. Judicial modesty, in short, must replace judicial arrogance. Sixteen years after he first explored these ideas in *Atherton*, Brandeis wrote his famous concurring opinion in *Ashwander* v. *TVA*, in effect codifying the various rules developed by the advocates of judicial

17. Alexander Bickel, *The Unpublished Opinions of Mr. Justice Brandeis* (Chicago: Univ. of Chicago Press, 1967), pp. 13–14. After holding the case for two terms without issuing an opinion, the Court finally declared the case moot. By this time the boy had reached the age of sixteen, and his continued employment would no longer trigger the application of the tax.

restraint to avoid constitutional decisions in cases unquestionably within the Court's jurisdiction:

> The Court will not pass upon the constitutionality of legislation in a friendly, non-adversary, proceeding. . . . The Court will not "anticipate a question of constitutional law in advance of the necessity of deciding it." . . . The Court will not "formulate a rule of constitutional law broader than is required by the precise facts to which it is to be applied." . . . The Court will not pass upon a constitutional question . . . if there is also present some other ground upon which the case may be disposed of. . . . The Court will not pass upon the validity of a statute upon complaint of one who fails to show that he is injured by its operation. . . . The Court will not pass upon the constitutionality of a statute at the instance of one who has availed himself of its benefits. . . . "When the validity of an act of the Congress is drawn in question, and even if a serious doubt of constitutionality is raised, it is a cardinal principle this Court will first ascertain whether a construction of the statute is fairly possible by which the question may be avoided."[18]

With Justices Holmes and Brandeis providing leadership from the high court and academics like Frankfurter training a new generation of lawyers, judicial restraint coupled with strict application of the rules of justiciability emerged as the defining characteristic of judicial liberalism and progressive politics on the eve of the New Deal.

Judicial Modesty Triumphant

The election of Franklin Roosevelt in 1932 and the explosion of legislative activity during the first hundred days of his administration fanned the flames of the controversy surrounding the proper role of the judiciary. A conservative majority on the Court continued in the tradition of activism in defense of property, but economic emergency and increased public demands for government action placed this understanding of the judicial role in serious jeopardy. As the eco-

18. 297 U.S. 288 at 346 (1936).

nomic and political crisis deepened, judicial activism increasingly came to be seen as the old order's most effective tool for checking reform and regulation despite overwhelming popular support for government action. In 1936 the Court actively employed judicial review to veto federal and state legislation designed to combat the depression, while in the November election Roosevelt won a stunning reelection victory. With the battle lines between the judiciary and the popularly elected branches starkly drawn, FDR in 1937 announced his plan to "pack" the Court with additional justices.[19] The motives behind the plan were apparent to all. Although the proposed legislation was never enacted by Congress, judicial retirement and death soon presented Roosevelt with the opportunity to transform the Supreme Court.

The Roosevelt appointees—a total of eight nominated and easily confirmed between 1937 and 1943—were all heirs to the tradition of restraint championed by Holmes and Brandeis. To a man, these justices came to the Court with a mandate to diminish the scope of judicial intervention in the policy-making arena and with an abiding faith that deference to the economic and social decisions of the elected branches would in the long run best serve the needs of the nation. With the judiciary in glorious retreat, liberalism emerged triumphant and judicial deference to Congress and the executive became an integral part of the New Deal's legacy to future generations. Thus the passion for judicial restraint that reached its zenith during the New Deal was born not of a fear of state power but of an appreciation of it, and the confining of judicial activism was a mark of liberal reform and not of conservative counterreaction.

A general acceptance of the jurisprudence of restraint and the limited institutional role of the judiciary united the judges and lawyers

---

19. The proposal would have permitted the president to appoint one new justice for each sitting justice who, upon reaching the age of seventy, declined to retire. The maximum number of judges on the Court would have been set at fifteen. In short, Roosevelt's plan would have permitted a president to name from one to six new justices, depending on how many sitting justices had reached the age of seventy and refused to step down.

of the New Deal. Even those championing a more active role in the protection of civil liberties paid homage to the model of restraint, seeking only to carve out a narrow exception to protect against majoritarian abuses of the democratic process.[20] Many prominent New Dealers later taught at the nation's most prestigious law schools, and the lessons they passed on to their students stressed the importance of a strong president and judicial deference to the elected branches. The saga of FDR's confrontation with the Supreme Court and the constitutional battles that marked the New Deal soon transcended mere history and became, in effect, a set of parables used to instruct future generations about the proper balance among the branches. The modern state, it was said, functioned best when a triumphant president could lead a submissive Congress in quest of enlightened policies. The received wisdom was equally unequivocal in demanding of the judiciary acceptance of the self-imposed limitations on the exercise of judicial review; to liberals whose political truths were formed during the era of the New Deal, judicial activism was simply incompatible with progressive politics. Their mission in the following decades was to ensure that this lesson was not lost on the generations that followed.[21]

For a brief period the Roosevelt Court functioned smoothly and without rancor, the shared belief in judicial deference to the elected branches being the unifying theme. By 1943 good will was, for the most part, long past and the Court was divided by personal disputes and ideological splits. Frankfurter was often at the heart of these divisions. His habit of lecturing his fellow justices much as he did his

20. The classic statement remains that of Justice Stone in *United States* v. *Carolene Products Co.*, 304 U.S. 144, 152, no. 4. See text accompanying note 47, infra.

21. The impact of generational change on the New Deal's understanding of judicial liberalism is explored in several essays by Martin Shapiro. See his "Fathers and Sons: The Court, the Commentators and the Search for Values," in Vincent Blasi, ed., *The Burger Court: The Counter-Revolution That Wasn't* (New Haven: Yale Univ. Press, 1983); "The Supreme Court: From Warren to Burger," in Anthony King, ed., *The New American Political System* (Washington, D.C.: AEI Press, 1978); "The Supreme Court and Economic Rights," in M. Judd Harmon, ed., *Essays on the Constitution of the United States* (Port Washington, N.Y.: Kennikat Press, 1978).

law students, coupled with a willingness to personalize any dispute, strained relations among the brethren. The justices of the Roosevelt Court remained firm in their acceptance of deference to the elected branches on matters of economic and social policy, but the unexpected rush of cases involving individual rights and liberties during World War II and thereafter shattered the ideological consensus of the justices. Frankfurter continued in his dedication to self-restraint, while Justice Hugo Black became the titular leader of a group advocating a more positive judicial role in the protection of individual rights.[22] Although this conflict divided the justices, it did not thrust the Court into open confrontation with the other branches. By the 1960s, however, judicial modesty and the active defense of civil liberties would prove to be essentially incompatible.

THE WARREN COURT

The Court and Its Critics

The triumph of the New Deal and the ideal of judicial restraint rendered the politics of judicial confirmations rather mundane. A vacancy on the Supreme Court might still produce partisan, insider wrangling, but as America approached midcentury the distinguished and the mediocre found their way to the Court with confirmation proceedings that were—at least by today's standards—little more than formalities. The federal judiciary's acceptance of its limited institutional role meant that the federal courts would no longer intervene in policy matters close to the heart of the New Deal, and the slowly emerging activism in the area of personal rights was in basic accord with the philosophy of the New Deal and did not seriously challenge executive power and prerogative. With the liberalism of the New

22. By the early 1940s Frankfurter was referring to Black and his supporters on the Court—William Douglas, Wiley Rutledge, and Frank Murphy—as "the Axis." See Silverstein, *Constitutional Faiths*, for a description of the different paths taken by Black and Frankfurter.

Deal ascendant, the political profile of the federal courts receded and the judiciary returned to a secondary position in determining the direction and fate of national policy.

From this perspective the appointment of Earl Warren as chief justice in 1953 marked a turning point in the history of the Supreme Court, surpassed in significance only by John Marshall's appointment 152 years earlier.[23] Renouncing the modest judicial role propounded by the theorists of the New Deal, the Court under Warren's leadership embraced the tradition of judicial assertiveness that began with the great Marshall. Marshall had established the possibility of extraordinary judicial power when judicial activism could be linked to the interests of powerful social, economic, and political forces. The crisis of the old order had been set in motion by a judicial arrogance founded on the mistaken belief that the resolute exercise of judicial review could withstand the dominant political impulses of the times. The justices of the Warren Court were not nearly so presumptuous. They set out to employ the federal judicial power to serve the interests of important components of the New Deal governing coalition, particularly America's ethnic and religious minorities. By linking the federal judiciary with Kennedy's New Frontier and Johnson's Great Society, the justices of the Warren Court were confident that judicial activism in the service of the disadvantaged would be embraced as the new definition of judicial liberalism.

The Court's return to an unabashed activism was not without controversy. Criticism from traditional conservative interests was expected and not particularly troublesome. Censure from the liberal

---

23. At the time of his appointment by President Dwight Eisenhower, Warren was in his third term as governor of California. He had previously served fourteen years as the district attorney for Alameda County and one term as the state attorney general. In the 1948 presidential election he had been John Dewey's running mate and had been seriously considered as a Republican presidential candidate in 1952. Surprising many (including the president who appointed him), Warren became the leader of the new liberal activism of the Supreme Court. This may have sorely disappointed the Republican Eisenhower, but history's assessment of Earl Warren is far kinder; Warren is considered to be one of the Court's great justices. For a sympathetic biography see G. Edward White, *Earl Warren: A Public Life* (New York: Oxford Univ. Press, 1982).

community struck much closer to home. Throughout the era of the Warren Court, a steady stream of criticism emanated from the pens of many prominent scholars whose understandings of the proper role of the judiciary had been honed during the battles of the Roosevelt presidency.[24] These critics condemned judicial activism in the modern democratic state even if the efforts of the Warren Court furthered many policies and substantive goals championed by the critics. The problem was not *what* the Court was doing but that it was a *court* that was doing it. Even a redemptive decision like *Brown* v. *Board of Education* was not immune from criticism; in the words of Professor Kurland, the desegregation decisions illustrated the hubris of the Warren justices in forgetting that "the Court, by itself, is incapable of effecting fundamental changes in society."[25] Martin Shapiro, who has written extensively of the impact of the New Deal on modern judicial review, captures the irony of the situation perfectly: "To an outsider, it often seemed wondrous indeed that so much energy was expended in seeking to persuade a particular organ of government not to act to achieve a goal that the would-be persuader was so anxious that other parts of government achieve."[26]

At this point the real judicial revolution wrought by the Warren Court comes into sharper focus. Whatever the controversy triggered by the desegregation cases or the decisions extending the protections of the Bill of Rights to state criminal proceedings, the core of the insurrection was the Court's rejection of the New Deal ideal of judicial modesty.[27] The New Deal judicial theorists had painstakingly formu-

24. A classic example of such scholarship is Philip Kurland, *Politics, the Constitution, and the Warren Court* (Chicago: Univ. of Chicago Press, 1970). See also Alexander Bickel, *The Supreme Court and the Idea of Progress* (New Haven: Yale Univ. Press, 1978). An article by Robert Bork, much discussed during his Senate confirmation hearings, broadly fits this description. See his "Neutral Principles and Some First Amendment Problems," *Indiana Law Journal* 47 (1971): 1.

25. 347 U.S. 483 (1954); Kurland, *Politics, the Constitution, and the Warren Court,* p. 113.

26. Shapiro, "Fathers and Sons," p. 219. See other citations in n. 21, supra.

27. The debate over whether any or all of the provisions of the Bill of Rights limited state governments began with the passage of the Fourteenth Amendment and continued with varying degrees of intensity through much of the twentieth century. See

lated the rules of justiciability and jurisdiction to narrow the sphere of judicial influence and free the elected branches from judicial domination. Disregarding the admonitions of this earlier generation of liberals that judicial power was essentially destructive of progressive politics, the justices of the Warren Court systematically ignored the complex web of rules designed to limit the exercise of judicial review; in so doing, they thrust the Supreme Court and the federal judiciary once again into the center of American politics.

Baker v. Carr and the Demise of the Political-Question Doctrine

Although Earl Warren came to the chief justiceship in 1953, the Warren Court did not reach full speed until the mid-1960s. Even the famous 1954 *Brown* decision did not begin to suggest the sweeping changes in the nature of judicial power that would take place in the next decade. It was not until the 1962 decision in *Baker* v. *Carr*, a case raising the difficult legal and potentially divisive question of whether malapportioned state legislatures violated the Constitution, that the real measure of the impending judicial revolution became readily evident.[28]

With the end of the Civil War began the great migration to America's cities. This general demographic trend, however, was not reflected in the makeup of most legislative and congressional districts in the nation. By the turn of the century, urban and suburban voters

---

Henry Abraham, *Freedom and the Court*, 5th ed. (New York: Oxford Univ. Press, 1988), chap. 3, for a brief history. The Warren Court's principal contribution was in the area of criminal procedure, applying to state criminal proceedings the Fourth Amendment search-and-seizure provisions, in *Mapp* v. *Ohio*, 367 U.S. 43 (1961); the Fifth Amendment's protections against self-incrimination, in *Malloy* v. *Hogan*, 378 U.S. 1 (1964), and double jeopardy, in *Benton* v. *Maryland*, 395 U.S. 784 (1969); the Sixth Amendment's guarantees of a jury trial, in *Duncan* v. *Louisiana*, 391 U.S. 145 (1968); confrontation, in *Pointer* v. *Texas*, 380 U.S. 400 (1965), counsel, *Gideon* v. *Wainwright*, 372 U.S. 335 (1963); and speedy trial, in *Klopfer* v. *North Carolina*, 386 U.S. 213 (1967); and the Eighth Amendment ban on cruel and unusual punishments, in *Robinson* v. *California*, 370 U.S. 660 (1962). The excerpts from the Fortas hearings in chapter 1 are striking examples of the controversy these decisions engendered.

28. 369 U.S. 186 (1962).

were seriously underrepresented in the state legislatures as well as in the House of Representatives. Since most state legislators were predictably unwilling to alter the electoral systems that placed them in office, those seeking to stem the disenfranchisement of urban voters sought judicial relief. State courts, however, often proved hesitant in ordering meaningful changes in the makeup of legislatures, and litigants who pursued similar claims in federal courts were met with a holding that the constitutionality of malapportioned legislatures was a political question and therefore nonjusticiable.

The political-question doctrine remains a fundamental example of a prudential rule intended to ensure that the federal courts avoid unnecessary conflict with other units of government. Stated much too simply for its complexity to be captured, the doctrine requires a federal court to refuse to rule on an issue properly before the court upon a determination that such an issue is unsuitable for judicial resolution. A claim that a particular issue constitutes a political question requires a court to determine whether it has the institutional competence to render judgment. A favorite of New Deal advocates of judicial modesty, the doctrine enables judges to avoid unnecessary clashes with the other branches and to soften the impact of the power of judicial review on the democratic process, by holding that particular issues are not amenable to judicial determination and better resolved by the other branches of government.[29]

For many years the apportionment of seats in state legislatures and congressional districting was considered just such a political question. During the 1940s, for example, Illinois congressional districts varied in population from 112,116 to 914,053. When neither the state legislature nor the state courts showed any willingness to re-

29. The term "political question" often confuses neophytes in the at times arcane world of constitutional law. Because virtually every constitutional decision rendered by a federal court has political implications, relying on everyday parlance might lead one to believe that every constitutional issue presents a potential "political question." In the field of constitutional law, however, "political question" has a specialized meaning, although any attempt to nail down a precise definition is bound to fail. For an interesting essay on the political-question doctrine, see Louis Henkin, "Is There a Political Question Doctrine?" *Yale Law Journal* 85 (1976): 597.

dress the imbalance, a federal lawsuit was filed contending that the disparity in the size of Illinois congressional districts ran afoul of the U.S. Constitution. In *Colegrove* v. *Green*, Justice Frankfurter, writing for a four-judge plurality, denied relief, asserting that the Constitution conferred upon Congress the authority to guarantee fair representation in the House.[30] Although the federal courts had the jurisdiction (that is, the power and authority to decide the matter), judicial respect for the authority of another branch of government and the frank acknowledgment of the judiciary's limited competence in these matters compelled the conclusion that this was an issue best left unresolved by the federal courts. "Due regard for the effective working of our Government," Frankfurter noted, "revealed this issue to be of a particularly political nature and therefore not for judicial determination." He concluded with his soon to be famous warning: "Courts ought not to enter this political thicket."

Frankfurter's conclusion in *Colegrove* that apportionment was a political question and thus nonjusticiable is hardly surprising; it is entirely consistent with the dominant New Deal philosophy that a passive judiciary would best serve the needs of progressive politics. Finding that the case presented a political question permitted the Court to dispose of a difficult, politically charged issue without facing the Hobson's choice of holding the shamefully malapportioned Illinois scheme constitutionally valid or invalidating it and assuming the herculean task of measuring the democratic legitimacy of every elected body at the national, state, and local level. Hardly a champion of legislatures weighted to favor rural interests, Frankfurter nonetheless believed *Colegrove* to be an example of farsighted decision making, certainly consistent with the teachings of Holmes and Brandeis. Not only would judicial intervention deny the elected branches the primary responsibility for progressive change, but the perilous task of deciding what constituted fair representation might ultimately subject the federal judiciary to serious political reprisals.

Sixteen years later Frankfurter's continual admonitions regard-

30. 328 U.S. 549, 552 (1946).

ing the teachings of Holmes and Brandeis and the lessons of the New Deal found a less receptive audience among his brethren on the Court. In March of 1962 the Court, over his vehement protests, essentially swept away the constraints of the political-question doctrine, holding in *Baker* v. *Carr* that the issue of malapportioned legislatures presented a justiciable claim under the equal-protection clause. Since 1901 not one reapportionment law had been passed in Tennessee, and, with urban voters seriously underrepresented in the state legislature, the plaintiffs in *Baker* sought a federal court decree holding the Tennessee apportionment scheme unconstitutional. A lower federal court dismissed the claim on the basis of *Colegrove.* In reversing and finding the issue of apportionment to be appropriate for judicial consideration, Justice Brennan's lengthy majority opinion marked the demise of the political-question doctrine as a significant limit on judicial power. In an internal memo to the chief justice and to Justices Black and Douglas, Brennan explained the necessity of his extended discussion of the political-question doctrine in the *Baker* opinion. "[A]fter much thought," he wrote, "I believe that the full discussion of 'political question,' and its bearing on apportionment suits, is required if we are effectively and finally to dispel the fog of another day produced by Felix's opinion in Colegrove v. Green."[31] The "fog of another day"—that is, the abiding faith that the judiciary could best serve progressive politics by playing an essentially secondary role—was at odds with a new model of government that partnered an activist judiciary with a dynamic executive branch in the quest to redefine American politics.

Immediately following the announcement of the result in *Baker*, two events occurred that proved to be turning points in the history of the Warren Court. Frankfurter had warned that entering the political thicket of reapportionment would expose the Court to a political backlash that the judiciary was ill equipped to resist. Such fears, however, proved groundless when the White House embraced the

31. Bernard Schwartz, *Super Chief: Earl Warren and His Supreme Court—A Judicial Biography* (New York: New York Univ. Press, 1983), pp. 419–20.

outcome in *Baker.* Equality of representation, President Kennedy noted in a news conference, was basic to a democracy, and the attorney general, Robert Kennedy, also publicly defended the decision.[32] When the debate over reapportionment sharpened, presidential support for the judiciary permitted the courts to weather the storm, and the reapportionment of the nation's legislatures took place with very little damage to the federal courts. Apart from the dire warnings of Justice Frankfurter, the lesson of the reapportionment cases appeared to be that judicial activism, when linked to presidential politics and constituencies, could serve the cause of progressive politics.

The second event was of still greater import. Within days of the decision in *Baker* v. *Carr*, Frankfurter suffered a debilitating stroke and, in August of 1962, formally announced his retirement from the Court. In his twenty-three years of service, he had been the Court's most vocal and articulate (and, at times, most irritating and pedantic) champion of a jurisprudence of restraint. Justices Hugo Black and William Douglas, the remaining Roosevelt appointees, continued to serve, but their vision of the Court as a powerful nationalizing force in American politics was diametrically opposite to that of Frankfurter. Others would continue the battle for judicial restraint, but Frankfurter's departure snapped the Court's last remaining link with the New Deal ideal of judicial deference.[33] The Warren Court revolution was about to gather steam.

32. Following the decision in *Baker* v. *Carr*, Dean Acheson, a Frankfurter friend, asked Kennedy what he thought about the decision. Acheson reported the president as saying "that legislatures would never reform themselves and that he did not see how we were going to make any progress unless the Court intervened." Quoted ibid, p. 425. Robert C. Cortner discusses the response to the reapportionment cases in his *The Apportionment Cases* (Knoxville: Univ. of Tennessee Press, 1970), pp. 176–77.

33. Saying that Frankfurter's retirement from the Court hastened the activism of the Warren Court is not meant to suggest that the voice of restraint was now absent from the Court. Justice John Harlan, for example, quickly emerged as Frankfurter's intellectual heir and as a superb advocate of restraint. Harlan, however, lacked Frankfurter's all-consuming passion, as well as his irritating manner, and the Court functioned quite smoothly with Harlan as the spokesman of the loyal opposition.

The Real Warren Court Revolution

In August of 1962 President Kennedy nominated his secretary of labor, Arthur Goldberg, to fill the Frankfurter seat. Easily confirmed by the Senate, Goldberg remained a justice of the Supreme Court for only three years. In 1965, at the behest of Lyndon Johnson, he resigned to become U.S. ambassador to the United Nations, and Johnson named Abe Fortas as his successor. The addition of Goldberg and then of Fortas solidified a working majority on the Court in favor of expanding federal judicial power to its constitutional limits. The chief justice's announced retirement in 1968 and the failure of the Fortas nomination marked the beginning of the end of this coalition, but, in the six years between Frankfurter's retirement and the Fortas hearings, the Court redefined liberal assumptions concerning judicial power and in a profound, albeit indirect, way altered the politics of judicial confirmations.

Baker signaled what was to follow; within months of Frankfurter's departure an energized Supreme Court resumed the campaign to dismantle the lattice of rules erected by the progressive jurists of the 1930s and 1940s to restrain judicial power. In short order the warnings of Brandeis in *Atherton* and *Ashwander* became quaint reminders of a bygone era. For example, the abstention doctrine provides that a federal court should decline to exercise jurisdiction and decide a constitutional issue when there are questions of state law that are unsettled and may be dispositive of the case. Although the federal courts have the power to rule on both the constitutional and the state law questions, the proper course for the cautious federal jurist is to abstain while the parties litigate the state claims in state court. Resolution of the state law issues in the state courts may prove dispositive and make the federal court proceedings unnecessary. The doctrine in the 1940s and 1950s loomed as a significant weapon for avoiding constitutional issues linked to cases clearly within the jurisdiction of the federal courts.[34] With the retirement of Frankfurter the doctrine

34. For example, in *Harrison* v. *NAACP*, 360 U.S. 167 (1959), the Court invoked the abstention doctrine to avoid reaching the constitutional merits of a claim that Virginia

became, in the words of one law review commentator, a "judicial orphan" in the Court's haste to secure federal court adjudication of important constitutional rights.[35]

The Court's interpretation of the limits imposed by the standing-to-sue doctrine provides another important example. The standing doctrine directs a court's attention to whether the particular party seeking relief has a sufficient stake in the outcome of the litigation to justify judicial resolution of the controversy. At a minimum, federal courts require a plaintiff to show "injury in fact" and that the injury is the result of the conduct challenged in the lawsuit. Deciding precisely what makes up the requisite injury and how close the nexus between the injury and the complained-of conduct must be has been the subject of countless litigation and scholarly commentaries. To the jurist schooled in the judicial liberalism of the New Deal, limiting access to the federal courts through strict application of the standing doctrine is an important technique for avoiding difficult and perhaps unnecessary constitutional decisions.

In 1943, for example, the Court denied a Connecticut physician standing to challenge a state statute prohibiting the use, or assistance in the use, of contraceptive devices, because the physician asserted that the statute infringed the constitutional rights of his patients who were not party to the case.[36] The complaint failed to allege any injury to the doctor, and therefore the majority concluded he lacked the requisite interest in the outcome to satisfy the requirements of the standing doctrine. When, in 1961, a husband and wife and their doctor sought a declaration that the same statute was invalid, Justice

---

statutes regulating lobbying and litigation efforts by organized groups were being employed to harass the NAACP. A majority concluded that the Virginia courts might possibly construe the statues in such a manner as to avoid the necessity of a constitutional ruling. The NAACP was required to file a new action in Virginia state court and, following a set of adverse rulings there, return to the Supreme Court, which ultimately ruled in its favor, *NAACP v. Button,* 371 U.S. 415 (1963). The four-year delay was simply considered a price paid for federalism and the need to restrain the exercise of judicial review.

35. See Note, "Federal-Question Abstention: Justice Frankfurter's Doctrine in an Activist Era," *Harvard Law Review* 80 (1967): 604.

36. *Tileston v. Ullman,* 318 U.S. 44 (1943).

Frankfurter, writing for the Court, again avoided a decision on the merits, by emphasizing that because the Connecticut statute had never been enforced against similar plaintiffs, the case was a hypothetical one and not appropriate for adjudication by the federal courts.[37] A decision on the constitutional merits of the Connecticut anti-birth-control law finally came in 1965 in *Griswold* v. *Connecticut*, where the Warren Court, undeterred by concerns of judicial vulnerability, swept aside any justiciability problems and held the statute invalid, recognizing for the first time a constitutional right of privacy.[38] By the mid-1960s the activist core of the Warren Court had relaxed the requirements of the standing doctrine to give a wide assortment of litigants the opportunity for a federal court determination of their constitutional claims.

The Court's rulings on abstention and standing as well as the other rules of justiciability, according to Professor Laurence Tribe, provide a "description of an institutional psychology: an account of how . . . the Justices of the Supreme Court view their own role."[39] In the case of the Warren Court, the role was that of an active partner with the executive branch in the transformation of American politics. The erosion of the judicially created limitations on judicial power expanded the reach of the federal judiciary, enhancing the opportunity of the courts to promote a new social and political agenda. In 1966, for instance, the Court amended Rule 23 of the Federal Rules of Civil Procedure to facilitate class action suits and thereby increased access to the federal courts for group litigants. To virtually no one's surprise, civil rights cases made up the vast majority of new class actions as the Court championed the causes of the racial and ethnic minorities of America, fusing the bond between the judiciary and the 1960s variant of the New Deal coalition.

All of this was a bit too much for those whose intellectual ties

37. *Poe* v. *Ullman*, 367 U.S. 497 (1961). Frankfurter's opinion quoted extensively from the Brandeis opinion in *Ashwander*. Four justices dissented.

38. 381 U.S. 579 (1965).

39. Laurence Tribe, *American Constitutional Law*, 2d ed. (Mineola, N.Y.: Foundation Press, 1988), p. 68.

to the jurisprudence of the New Deal remained intact. "The [Warren] Court has substantially loosened the definition of a lawsuit," lamented Alexander Bickel, Frankfurter's most brilliant protégé; "it has opened the door wider to more litigants and has indeed come near to making the lawsuit something of a formality, still an expensive one, but within the reach of just about all who can afford it, at just about any time of their choice."[40] In Bickel's view the *unmistakable* lesson of the New Deal era was that expansion of the judicial role was incompatible with lasting reform and would ultimately threaten the institutional independence of the judiciary. To the justices of the Warren Court, however, throwing off the shackles of a constricted view of the Court's power simply brought a greater diversity of litigants before the Court and rendered a wider range of issues subject to judicial determination.

Easing the rules governing justiciability was not the only transgression of the Warren Court, in the view of those who supported the model of judicial modesty; among its other sins they counted its opinion-writing technique and its eagerness to expand the nature and scope of judicial remedies. Brandeis in *Ashwander* urged the justices to focus their attention narrowly and render judgment only on questions necessary to the outcome of the case. Avoiding broad constitutional decrees, it was thought, would lessen the potential conflict between the federal judiciary and the democratic system, reserving most issues for resolution by majority rule. As the Warren revolution progressed, this admonition was all but forgotten, for the Court often moved beyond simply deciding a case and delivered broad and sometimes controversial policy pronouncements. The important decision in the 1966 case of *Miranda v. Arizona* provides a convenient example.[41]

Ernesto Miranda had been arrested and taken to a police interrogation room and, without being advised of his right to have an attorney present, questioned for several hours. At his trial on charges

40. Bickel, *Supreme Court*, p. 108.
41. 384 U.S. 436 (1966).

of rape and kidnaping, Miranda's statements to the police were admitted into evidence, over the objection of his attorney. The basic issue presented in *Miranda* and its companion cases was whether self-incriminating statements made without full warning of the suspect's constitutional rights could be used at trial to secure a conviction. In a 5-to-4 decision, the Court held the statements inadmissible. Assigned the task of crafting the majority opinion, a proponent of judicial modesty might have carefully fashioned a narrow opinion closely tailored to the facts of the case, relying on future cases to develop incrementally a comprehensive set of constitutional rules governing the questioning of criminal suspects. Chief Justice Warren's opinion, however, seized the opportunity to establish a detailed code of police behavior designed to govern all future police-suspect confrontations. Thirty-two pages of the opinion were dedicated to the discussion and formulation of the famous *Miranda* warnings—the explicit statement of the suspect's rights that henceforth would be required to be given to the suspect prior to police interrogation—while less than nine pages dealt with the constitutional authority for the result. Furthermore, by holding that some newly announced constitutional standards applied only prospectively, the Warren Court bypassed a very real inhibition on the Court's willingness to alter rules of criminal procedure.[42]

The explosion of public law litigation and litigants in the 1960s created the need for innovative remedies to effectuate the expanded judicial role. The transition from a judiciary primarily engaged in resolving private disputes to one confronting many of the most pressing and intractable of society's problems required a change in the

42. Consider the problem presented by *Miranda*. The Court's alteration of the constitutional standards of police-suspect confrontations would naturally trigger a subsequent case contending that a prisoner who did not receive the proper warnings—even though tried and convicted before the decision in *Miranda*—should be entitled to a habeas corpus hearing and perhaps release from prison. The prospect of thousands of hearings and retrials for convicted prisoners imposes an enormous constraint on a Court contemplating a change in the constitutional rules of criminal procedure. Holding that *Miranda* applied only prospectively—see *Johnson* v. *New Jersey*, 384 U.S. 719 (1966)—freed the Court from this constraint.

nature and scope of judicial decrees.[43] The Warren Court encouraged judges throughout the federal system to fashion innovative remedies that often required public officials to implement complex and varied policies designed by the court to square the defendant's practices with constitutional requirements. As a result, federal courts assumed the day-to-day operation of public schools, prisons, public housing, and state mental institutions. By the 1970s the federal judiciary had carved out the power to detail the manner in which other governmental units would conduct their business and was thus able to provide successful litigants with remedies similar to those previously available only through the executive or legislative branches.[44]

The most striking decisions of the Warren era—the desegregation cases, the efforts to enlarge the protections afforded by the First Amendment, and the continued nationalization of the Bill of Rights—remain that Court's most important legacies. These were the decisions that captured the headlines, galvanizing the Court's supporters, infuriating its critics, and challenging a scholarly tradition skeptical of the judiciary's capacity to bring about redemptive social change. The substructure for this constitutional revolution was far less visible but no less significant and certainly as revolutionary. The arcane and complex world of justiciability standards and federal court jurisdiction did not lend itself to newspaper headlines or facile editorial commentary, but the Warren Court's work in these areas posed a weighty challenge to the old order. By the mid-1960s the advocates of judicial activism had no doubt that a dynamic federal judiciary could further progressive objectives, particularly by linking the fate of the disadvantaged and electorally powerless with that of the Court. A judiciary sensitive to the needs of racial, ethnic, and religious minorities, em-

---

43. See, for example, Phillip Cooper, *Hard Judicial Choices: Federal District Court Judges and State and Local Officials* (New York: Oxford Univ. Press, 1988); Donald Horowitz, *The Courts and Social Policy* (Washington, D.C.: Brookings Institution, 1970); Abram Chayes, "The Role of the Judge in Public Interest Litigation," *Harvard Law Review* 89 (1976): 1281.

44. For a conservative's critique of this development, see Gary McDowell, *Equity and the Constitution* (Chicago: Univ. of Chicago Press, 1982).

ploying the equal-protection clause and the First Amendment to simplify mass politics and communication, would also be assured the political support of the Kennedy and Johnson administrations. When asked, Earl Warren invariably pointed to *Baker* v. *Carr* as the Court's most important decision during his tenure as chief justice. *Baker* was not only the opening gambit in the Court's campaign to constitutionalize the "one man one vote" principle but also a direct assault on the citadel of judicial restraint and an unequivocal proclamation that the standards of justiciability would no longer stand as a bar to the Court's defense of enlightened self-government.

THE BURGER COURT AND BEYOND

A New Constituency for the Federal Courts

The failed Fortas nomination of 1968 symbolized the end of the Warren Court revolution, but the impact of the Warren years on the nature of judicial power survived the passing of the men who gave the revolution life. The jurists of the New Deal had hoped to harmonize judicial review with the needs of a modern, progressive society by obliging judges to observe a stringent assortment of restrictions on the exercise of judicial power. Shrinking the scope of judicial influence, they believed, would create greater constitutional space for the other branches to govern effectively. The Warren Court revolution of the mid-1960s constituted a frontal attack on this essentially passive understanding of the judicial role. The judicial theorist of the New Deal valued strict adherence to the rules of standing because rigorously confining who could properly invoke the jurisdiction of the federal courts would diminish the judiciary's impact on the political system. The justices of the Warren Court, however, liberalized the standing rules with precisely the opposite outcome in mind. Likewise, the political-question doctrine narrowed the range of issues federal courts could properly decide; disregarding it as a limitation broadened the capacity of the federal courts to pass judgment on novel claims.

Historically the exercise of judicial review had involved the exercise of a negative power, basically returning the parties to the situation that existed before the enforcement of the challenged government action. By the late 1960s decisions like *Miranda* and the development of new judicial remedies had made the federal courts active participants in reform, permitting judges to direct other political actors on precisely how to achieve the policy outcomes sought by the court.

In opening the doors of the federal courthouse to a multitude of new litigants and constitutional claims and providing potent remedies to those who prevailed, the justices of the Warren Court established the federal judiciary as a commanding force in the policy-making process. Whatever the merits of this development—and much may be said both pro and con—an unanticipated consequence was to make the selection of the men and women who would sit on the federal bench a matter of vast importance and concern to an array of groups and interests far wider than ever before in American history. The Fortas defeat was simply one of the first manifestations of the new state of affairs. The appointment of Warren Burger the following year as chief justice did not alter this new reality. Although Burger did not share his predecessor's soaring vision of the Court as the protector of the weak and disenfranchised, the Burger Court did not significantly tighten access to the federal court or surrender the tools of judicial power fashioned during the Warren era.[45]

Scholars have long recognized that groups unable to compete in

45. Although the Burger Court is generally considered more moderate in its actions than is its predecessor, it did not seriously alter the Warren Court's liberalized justiciability standards. See Bernard Schwartz, *The Ascent of Pragmatism: The Burger Court in Action* (Reading, Mass.: Addison-Wesley, 1990), chap. 2; William Atkin and Burton Taggart, "Substantive Access Doctrines and Conflict Management in the U.S. Supreme Court: Reflections on Activism and Restraint," in Stephen Halpern and Charles Lamb, eds., *Supreme Court Activism and Restraint* (Lexington, Mass.: Lexington Books, 1982). Although specific decisions, like Justice Powell's discussion of standing in *Warth* v. *Sedlin*, 422 U.S. 490 (1975), might contrast with efforts of the Warren Court, access to the federal courts was not significantly confined by the Burger Court, and the expansive decisions of the Warren era were not overruled. As a result, the current Court find itself in a uniquely powerful position, blessed with recent precedent that can be used to grant or deny litigants access to the federal courts without flagrant disregard for judicial standards.

the legislative or executive arena often turn to the courts for access to government power.[46] The first, tentative acknowledgment of a duty to act on behalf of such groups came from the Supreme Court in 1938.[47] By the 1960s the judicial obligation to the politically powerless had led to much of the activism of the Warren Court, including the drive to reexamine the justiciability standards. This "out-group" understanding of interest group litigation, however, fails to capture the Warren era's extraordinary impact on judicial power. Throwing the doors of the courthouse wide open and providing an extensive range of remedies to those who entered ultimately benefited not only the disadvantaged but many affluent, middle- and upper-middle-class interests. With the coming of the Burger Court, in the early 1970s, an assortment of these interests—for example, environmentalists, feminists, consumer groups, political reformers— found in the judiciary an attractive alternative to the other branches in the battle to secure their goals. Thirty years previously the majority of those groups seeking access to the federal courts may well have been the politically impotent; in the modern era, however, increased access to the courts has combined with the new tools of judicial power to make the judiciary an attractive ally for a host of powerful constituent groups.[48]

46. See Richard Cortner, "Strategies and Tactics of Litigation in Constitutional Cases," *Journal of Public Law* 17 (1968): 287.

47. *United States* v. *Carolene Products Co.*, 304 U.S. 144 (1938), was an unremarkable decision upholding a federal statute excluding "filled milk" from interstate commerce. It was based on the New Deal wisdom that the Court would not interfere with congressional decisions unless the legislature had acted without a rational basis. In the famous footnote 4 to that decision, however, Justice Stone suggested that judicial activism might be justified when (1) the legislation was within a specific prohibition of the Constitution (for example, the Bill of Rights), (2) the legislation restricted the ability of groups and individuals to influence the political process, and (3) the legislation was aimed at disadvantaging "discrete and insular minorities" unable to protect their interests in the political process.

48. This is not to suggest that comparatively affluent, progressive groups shunned court action prior to the late 1960s. During the early twentieth century the National Consumers League frequently appeared in court, often represented by Louis Brandeis and Felix Frankfurter in their pre-Court days, in litigation to improve working conditions. Typically, however, the NCL was engaged in *defensive* litigation to protect enacted

Roe v. *Wade* provides perhaps the starkest example of the Warren Court's impact on its allegedly more cautious successor.[49] There is little need to chronicle here the controversy engendered by *Roe* since the decision was announced, early in 1973. In the minds of those with degrees from the Frankfurter school of constitutional jurisprudence, the tumult was the result of yet another judicially self-inflicted wound, because in their view *Roe* was a case that cried out for judicial avoidance. In the years preceding *Roe* a significant reform movement advocating the liberalization of the nation's abortion laws appeared in several states. Between 1967 and 1973 nineteen states had reformed their abortion statutes, with New York, Hawaii, and Alaska repealing criminal restrictions through the twentieth week of a pregnancy.[50] The emergence of several important women's groups intensified the political debate; for example, the National Organization of Women was established in 1966 and a year later voted to include reproductive freedom in NOW's women's bill of rights. Although reform may not have been immediate or sweeping, by the early 1970s debate over abortion was part of mainstream American politics, and even the most sympathetic of judges might, in good faith, avoid reaching a difficult and novel constitutional issue in deference to the workings of the democratic system.

Abortion was, moreover, not an issue that lent itself to easy judicial resolution. Many of the nation's abortion statutes made performing an abortion a crime. The party directly affected was the doctor, but old justiciability decisions could be cited to bolster the conclusion that the doctor lacked standing to assert the constitutional rights of her patients. The claim of a pregnant woman that the Constitution guaranteed her the abortion choice might be met by a dismissal for mootness; none other than Brandeis himself had urged progressive jurists to pay particular attention to whether controver-

---

legislation against constitutional attack. See Clement Vose, "National Consumers League and the Brandeis Brief," *Midwest Journal of Political Science* 1 (1957): 267.

49. 410 U.S. 113 (1973).

50. See Laurence Tribe, *Abortion: The Clash of Absolutes* (New York: Norton, 1990), chap. 3, for a brief review of the history of restrictions on abortion in the United States.

sial cases posed a live, ongoing controversy and the human gestation period is far shorter than that of a constitutional case.[51] In short, the claim that the Constitution protected a woman's right to an abortion was precisely the type of case that a generation of judges had been schooled to avoid.

In both *Roe* and its companion case, *Doe* v. *Bolton*, pregnant women sought a declaration that state abortion laws were unconstitutional. The three-year delay between the filing of the cases and Supreme Court review meant that the cases could easily be found to be moot and subject to dismissal, because the petitioners no longer had a personal stake in their outcomes. Following in the tradition of the Warren Court, however, not one justice on the Burger Court gave more than a passing thought to avoiding this complex (not to mention politically divisive) constitutional issue through the expedient route of a dismissal for mootness.[52] Justice Blackmun's original draft opinion for the Court did attempt to achieve a similar outcome by holding that the Texas statute was too vague in describing when an abortion could and could not legally be performed.[53] Such a holding would have accomplished much the same as a dismissal for mootness: disposing of the case without a binding determination of the basic

51. The flip side of mootness is ripeness, another limitation imposed by standards of justiciability. Mootness asks whether the controversy that existed between the parties has been concluded, that is, whether there continues to exist a "live" controversy. Ripeness, on the other hand, demands that federal courts determine whether the controversy has become sufficiently focused and concrete to warrant judicial intervention. Very simply, a finding of mootness is a finding that judicial intervention is coming too late in the game, while the ripeness requirement asks whether it is coming too early. For an example of the cautious jurist attempting to use ripeness to avoid a constitutional issue, see Justice Frankfurter dissenting in *Adler* v. *Board of Education,* 342 U.S. 485 (1952).

52. At the first conference following the initial argument in *Roe,* all the justices agreed without much discussion that none of the possible justiciability arguments foreclosed a decision on the merits. Schwartz, *Ascent of Pragmatism,* p. 47.

53. Ibid., p. 301. A criminal statute is considered constitutionally "void for vagueness" when it fails to provide adequate notice of what behavior is considered criminal. The Texas statute permitted abortions "to save the life of the mother." Blackmun concluded that this criterion did not inform the physician whether an abortion could be performed only when the patient would certainly die without it or whether an abortion was permissible when there was simply a possibility that the patient would die without it.

issue of whether the constitution protected from state interference a woman's decision regarding abortion.

The circulation of the Blackmun draft opinion prompted Justices Douglas and Brennan immediately to respond with "Dear Harry" letters reminding Blackmun that a majority in the conference had voted to reach the core constitutional issue.[54] The reaction of Douglas and Brennan (who, along with Justice Thurgood Marshall, made up the Court's unreconstructed liberals) was perhaps to be expected; more enlightening was the fact that Blackmun's vagueness argument, like the mootness point, failed to attract any significant support among his other colleagues. Liberals and conservatives appeared equally disposed to confront the merits of the abortion claim. As a result, Justice Blackmun's majority opinion, issued a year later, simply dispenses with the justiciability problems in a few sentences.[55] The remainder of the opinion, following the *Miranda* technique, not only unequivocally establishes the constitutional protection for a woman's right to choose but describes at some length an elaborate, judicially created framework to govern state efforts to regulate abortion in the future.

Reaching the merits of a similar case in a similar posture would have been unthinkable twenty-five years earlier. A decade of increased access to the courts coupled with the emergence of a politically potent women's movement made the abortion issue palatable to the justices of the Burger Court. The Warren Court, in its quest to serve the disadvantaged, had opened the doors of the federal courthouse, and during the Burger years a multitude of interests, including upper-middle-class citizens and professional groups, marched right in.

54. Ibid., p. 303.
55. The one-year delay was a result of the deaths of Justices Black and Harlan. The initial deliberations in the abortion cases took place after Black and Harlan left the Court but prior to the confirmations of their replacements. After Blackmun filed his original draft opinion, several justices, including Blackmun and Chief Justice Burger, moved to have the cases held over and reargued to permit the new justices, Rehnquist and Powell, to participate. Thus *Roe* was actually argued twice, although the votes of the new justices did not affect the outcome, as Justice Powell joined Justice Blackmun's opinion and Justice Rehnquist filed a dissent.

Following *Roe*, groups such as NOW, the American Civil Liberties Union, the Women's Equity Action League, the Women's Legal Defense Fund, and Planned Parenthood devoted substantial time and effort to litigation in the federal courts in the effort to realize substantive goals broadly identified with the women's movement. Even groups not typically associated with court action—for example, the American Association of University Women and the League of Women Voters—were soon filing briefs and sponsoring litigation to further their particular policy agenda.[56] Their adroitness in using the federal courts provoked opposition groups like the Americans United for Life and the United States Catholic Conference to develop countervailing litigation strategies. Quite rapidly, federal courthouses became the principal battlefields in the war to define the depth and breadth of gender equality in the United States. To those who had kept the faith with the New Deal idea of restraint—regardless of their position on gender equality—this was precisely the outcome they had fought so hard to avoid.

Feminists and their rivals were, of course, not the only groups to focus attention of the federal courts. Indeed, during the years of the Burger Court the overall group presence in the federal judicial system increased substantially.[57] Although traditional business interests continued to be the most frequent participants, there was a marked increase in the participation rates of citizens' groups reflecting essentially middle- and upper-middle-class concerns. The expectations of the Warren Court notwithstanding, increased access, whether to the judiciary or to Congress, eventually benefits the affluent and the

56. See Tracy George and Lee Epstein, "Women's Rights Litigation in the 1980s: More of the Same?" *Judicature* 74 (1991): 314.

57. See Lee Epstein, "Courts and Interest Groups," in John B. Gates and Charles A. Johnson, *The American Courts: A Critical Assessment* (Washington, D.C.: CQ Press, 1991), for a discussion of the scholarly literature and data pointing to the increase in interest group activity during the last twenty years. Professor Epstein's essay also discusses the value of the amicus curiae brief to groups seeking to influence the Supreme Court. One measure of the increased use of the courts in the 1970s and 1980s might well be the escalating critical rhetoric of those clinging to the New Deal understanding of the role of the courts. In this vein see Richard Morgan, *Disabling America: The Rights Industry in Our Time* (New York: Basic, 1983).

educated. Thus beyond women's rights advocates, groups promoting consumer and environmental causes, for example, quickly established impressive litigation records during this period. Several commentators reviewing this period have noted that *organized* environmental interests, as opposed to individuals seeking redress for alleged environmental transgressions, found the federal courts particularly receptive to their claims.[58] The considerable body of environmental and consumer protection case law now on the books was nonexistent a mere thirty years ago, and the plethora of law school offerings in these subjects today is testimony to the willingness of the modern courts to consider novel claims on behalf of organized, affluent litigants.[59]

Another indicator of expanded group influence during the 1970s and 1980s is the explosive growth in the number of amicus curiae (friend of the court) briefs filed with the Supreme Court. The amicus brief was originally intended to offer a means by which a person or organization not party to a case could bring to the attention of the Court facts or legal matters that would not be adequately presented by the parties. Relatively easy and inexpensive to file, the amicus brief has in recent years proven to be an extremely popular medium for groups with an interest in the outcome of a particular case to register their preferences with the Court. For example, in the famous 1978 *Bakke* case, in which the Court confronted the controversial question of the constitutionality of affirmative action programs, 120 organizations joined in the filing of fifty-eight amicus briefs.[60] In the 1982 term of the Court, 1,400 organizations submitted or joined in the sponsoring of amicus briefs. By the 1987 term, amicus briefs were filed in 80

58. On the success of organized groups like the Sierra Club, as opposed to individual or ad hoc interests in environmental litigation, see Lettie M. Wenner, *The Environmental Decade in Court* (Bloomington: Univ. of Indiana Press, 1982), chap. 3.

59. "The environmental plaintiff of the 1970s found a sympathetic reception in the [federal] courts." J. William Futrell, "The Ungreening of the Court," *Environmental Forum*, Jan.–Feb. 1992, p. 13. Mr. Futrell places special emphasis on the willingness of the federal judiciary in the 1970s to interpret federal environmental statutes broadly, at times seemingly moving well beyond the apparent intent of Congress in enacting the measure.

60. *Regents of the University of California* v. *Bakke*, 438 U.S. 265 (1978).

percent of the cases decided by the Court on the merits.[61] This trend has continued uninterrupted. A not untypical 1991 case, *United Mine Workers* v. *Johnson Controls*, turned on the question of whether the Civil Rights Act of 1964 barred employers from excluding fertile women from jobs out of concern for the fetus the woman might conceive.[62] Participating through the amicus process were such disparate groups as the American Nurses Association, the National Resources Defense Council, and the United States Catholic Conference.

When groups broadly located on the left of the political spectrum (see the discussion of "New Progressives" in chapter 3) found the judiciary a sympathetic ally in the battle to secure policy goals, interests with a conservative agenda took steps to develop their own litigation program. The growth of conservative public-interest law firms and legal foundations, another phenomenon of the last two decades, is further testimony to the federal judiciary's increased significance to an entirely new set of interests.[63] When, during the early 1970s, several liberal groups sponsored litigation challenging then Governor Ronald Reagan's attempts to impose substantial cuts on the California welfare system, conservatives founded the Pacific Legal Foundation to provide a conservative counterpart to liberal public-interest law firms. The success of the Pacific Legal Foundation spawned other conservative litigation groups. The Mountain States Legal Foundation, for example, sponsored several important legal actions on behalf of conservative interests and supplied a pool of unabashedly conservative lawyers to Republican administrations.[64] The Capital Legal Foundation supported and litigated General Westmoreland's libel action against "60 Minutes" and the Columbia Broad-

61. Lawrence Baum, *The Supreme Court*, 4th ed. (Washington, D.C.: CQ Press, 1992), pp. 86–87.

62. 111 S. Ct. 1196 (1991).

63. See, for example, Lee Epstein, *Conservatives in Court* (Knoxville: Univ. of Tennessee Press, 1985).

64. For example, Mountain States provided the Reagan administration James Watt (secretary of the interior) and Rex Lee (solicitor general).

casting System. Without undue exaggeration it can be said that the federal courts now form a crucial theater of operations for a wide array of upper-middle-class interests seeking to use a receptive and activist judiciary to promote policy goals. What began as the Warren Court's effort to empower the underdogs now often serves the interests of the affluent and politically powerful.

Bork and Thomas and the Modern Confirmation Process

Simple observations often provide the most satisfactory explanations for complex phenomena. The crescendo of voices demanding to be heard in the modern confirmation process is in no small measure a by-product of the expanded role of the federal judiciary in late-twentieth-century America. The Warren Court altered not only the nature of judicial power but the nature of the confirmation process as well. Powerful groups from all points along the ideological spectrum now consider a sympathetic judiciary essential to the development and achievement of important policy goals. Nominations to the Supreme Court and, to a lesser degree, to the lower federal courts thus command the attention of a wide range of interests, provoke sophisticated campaigns to mobilize grassroots support, and trigger the expenditure of substantial sums of private money in the effort to sway public opinion. Given the expansion of judicial power and influence over the last three decades, it should hardly be surprising that the process of selecting and confirming federal judges increasingly resembles a national electoral campaign.

The clash over the nomination of Robert Bork to the Supreme Court offers the most distinctive example of the new politics of judicial power. For our limited purposes it is important not to lose sight of the fact that Judge Bork not only had unchallenged professional qualifications for the high court but also was one of his generation's most vocal (and prominent) critics of the activism of the Warren Court. This fact alone assured a substantial level of opposition to his nomination. Early on, opponents of the nomination set about to compile a collection of Bork's scholarly writings and his opinions while a judge on the U.S. Court of Appeals. Exposure to what came to be known as the "Book of Bork," it was thought, would energize numerous groups with no predisposition to oppose Bork but with a growing interest in the staffing of the federal judiciary.[65] For example, in a 1985 interview Bork asserted that an expansive understanding of the standing-to-sue doctrine "would so enhance the power of the courts as to make them the dominant branch of government." He concluded the interview as follows: "Every time a court expands the definition of standing, the definition of interests it is willing to protect through adjudication, the area of judicial dominance grows and the area of democratic rule contracts."[66]

The real task of the groups initially opposing Bork was to use his derision of the broad expansion of judicial power of the last several decades as the catalyst for propelling into the fray groups not normally associated with confirmation battles. During the course of the Bork proceedings, for example, the general counsel of the Audubon Society was moved to write the members of the Senate Judiciary Committee and illustrate how Bork's interpretation of the rules of standing and justiciability might seriously constrict the ability of citizen groups to challenge in federal court "the weakening of national surface mining regulations" or to require the government "to issue regulations protecting visibility in our national parks to protect some unique and threatened resources like Mono Lake, the Alaska Coastal Plain or whooping cranes in Central Nebraska."[67] Similar concerns united many organizations opposing Judge Bork. The alliance that formed in 1987 to defeat the nomination was extraordinary, if only because of the diversity of interests that united in a common endeavor.[68] Building an effective coalition with interests ranging from

65. Michael Pertschuk and Wendy Schaetzel, *The People Rising* (New York: Thunder's Mouth Press, 1989), chap. 3 of which describes the evolution and the content of the "Book of Bork."

66. Quoted in Patrick McGuigan and Dawn Weyrich, *Ninth Justice* (Washington, D.C.: Free Congress, 1990), p. 297.

67. Quoted in Pertschuk and Schaetzel *People Rising*, p. 184.

68. The number of groups campaigning to defeat Bork numbered in the neighborhood of three hundred. See ibid., appendix B, for a "representative sampling" of these groups.

the United Mine Workers to the National Gay and Lesbian Task Force is obviously no easy matter. In the Bork campaign the adhesive that bound these groups together was Bork's cramped conception of the role of the federal judiciary in modern America. In the 1960s the Warren Court's expansion of access to the federal courts was revolutionary; by the mid-1980s it was considered simply business as usual, and a vast array of interests was prepared to defend what was already part of the status quo. Bork was easily portrayed by his opponents as a radical conservative precisely because he was considered by many a threat to a dynamic and active federal judiciary.

The political moral of the Bork nomination battle is that there is a substantial reservoir of support for (or opposition to, for that matter) most nominees to the Court and that victory belongs to the side that most effectively mobilizes its active and potential supporters. Notwithstanding cries of foul by many passionate Bork supporters, his failed nomination was hardly the handiwork of a cabal of liberal activists, perverting the normal politics of judicial selection.[69] The roots of Bork's defeat reached back thirty years, to the activism of the Warren era, and the particular circumstances of the Bork nomination (a lame-duck and weakened Republican president, a particularly controversial nominee, a Senate controlled by Democrats) simply added fuel to an already raging fire. The nomination of Robert Bork was defeated because the opposition understood the reality of modern judicial confirmations better than did his supporters. Little wonder that an ardent Bork supporter and conservative activist vowed in the wake of the Bork defeat "to prepare for every confirmation battle to be the legislative equivalent of a senatorial campaign with high dollar media expenditures, vigorous negative advertising and polemical theatrics."[70]

The shattering defeat of Judge Bork energized the right wing of the Republican party. In the months following the failed nomination, organizations connected with the New Right searched out potential

---

69. See Suzanne Garment, "The War against Robert Bork," *Commentary*, Jan. 1988, pp. 17–26, for an example of the "liberal conspiracy/perversion of normal process" approach.

70. McGuigan and Weyrich, *Ninth Justice*, pp. 221–22.

candidates for judicial positions and began to develop strategies for securing their nomination and eventual confirmation.[71] Clarence Thomas was the product of just such a talent search. During his days as the head of the Equal Employment Opportunity Commission, Thomas met with several New Right organizations to assure them of the soundness of his views on the social and legal issues of the day. These same organizations actively promoted his appointment to the court of appeals in 1989 and two years later assisted in securing his nomination to succeed the retiring Justice Marshall on the Supreme Court. The Thomas nomination supplied conservative activists not simply with the long-awaited occasion to avenge the Bork defeat but also with the opportunity to carry out new strategies for judicial confirmation. Applying the lessons learned during the Bork defeat, conservative groups began a major fund-raising and lobbying campaign to secure Senate confirmation and energize grassroots support.[72] Pat Robertson's Christian Coalition, for example, spent over one million dollars on behalf of the Thomas nomination, producing a television ad said to have generated over 100,000 letters and telephone calls in his favor. On the other hand, the opposition was stymied; liberals went out of their way to "like" Clarence Thomas. As the Bush administration correctly calculated, his Horatio Alger success story and his race undercut opposition to the nomination.

The allegations of sexual harassment on the eve of the Senate confirmation vote transformed the confirmation of a Supreme Court justice into a revelatory moment in American history. Even before Anita Hill's testimony fascinated a worldwide audience, however, the

71. For a discussion of the New Right, see infra, chap. 3.

72. Timothy Phelps and Helen Winternitz, *Capitol Games: Clarence Thomas, Anita Hill, and the Story of a Supreme Court Nomination* (New York: Hyperion, 1992), details at some length the efforts of conservative groups on behalf of Thomas. Among these groups were Gary Bauer's Family Research Council, Phyllis Schafly's Eagle Forum, Beverly LaHaye's Concerned Women for America, the Reverend Louis Sheldon's Coalition for Traditional Values, and Pat Robertson's Christian Coalition. Although all these groups were united in their opposition to abortion, many reflected the extreme positions of the fringe radical Right. For example, La Haye's group does not accept any separation of church and state, arguing that government officials who do not use the Bible as their guide to public life do not belong in office.

Thomas nomination was of signal importance. In 1987 the New Progressives had engineered a major political campaign to defeat the nomination of Robert Bork, a man whose professional qualifications would at first blush have seemed to guarantee him a seat on the Court. Four years later the New Right activists masterminded a similar crusade to place on the Court an individual with embarrassingly meager professional qualifications and substantial links to fringe right-wing political groups. In part, the explanation for both these events lies in the changes in judicial power. But these changes over the last several decades must also be placed in the context of developments in the larger political setting. The fragmentation of the New Deal coalition during the 1960s and 1970s and the tensions inherent in the Republican majority of the 1980s enhanced the potential rewards for groups adept at cultivating new forums for the enactment and implementation of policy goals. In a political environment marked by "gridlock" and fragmented national parties, the stakes surrounding judicial appointments rise rather quickly. It is to these developments at the "macro level" of national politics that we now turn.

Chapter 3

THE DEMOCRATS: THE COMING
OF THE NEW PROGRESSIVES

From the days of the New Deal through the fateful election of 1968, the Democratic party set the tone and direction of American political life. With the Roosevelt coalition in place, attention focused on the building of a powerful administrative state, and appointments to the federal courts, even at the level of the Supreme Court, excited only minimal investigation and public interest. The dissolution of this coalition, however, altered not only American politics on the grand scale but the process of judicial selection and confirmation as well. The passing of Democratic hegemony forced elements of the party to seek alternative forums and means for the achievement of their policy agenda. Beginning in the late 1960s an activist judiciary emerged as an important institutional ally of powerful groups associated with the Democratic party, thereby substantially raising the political stakes in the selection and confirmation of Supreme Court justices.

THE DEMISE OF THE NEW DEAL COALITION

The Legacy of the New Deal

In the years following the New Deal, the legacy of Franklin Roosevelt shaped national political life, and the Democratic party emerged as the dominant political force in the United States.[1] Democrats far outnumbered Republicans; in 1954, 46 percent of the electorate iden-

1. William E. Leuchtenburg, *In the Shadow of FDR: From Harry Truman to Ronald Reagan* (Ithaca: Cornell Univ. Press, 1983).

tified with the Democratic party, compared with 34 percent who considered themselves Republicans.[2] The New Deal produced a new public philosophy that transformed the relationship between the citizen and the national government. For the first time in the history of the Republic, the federal government assumed primary responsibility for the redistribution of wealth and the regulation of economic life.[3] The resulting growth in the size and responsibilities of the centralized government during this period furthered Democratic hegemony by linking the interests of a diverse mass constituency to the party through the development of a host of federal programs administered by an expanding executive branch. The electorate accepted Washington, D.C., as the guardian of the economic and social well-being of the country and the Democratic party as the prime proponent of national action to solve the nation's domestic problems.

To compete successfully, Republicans were forced to acknowledge the reality of America's limited welfare state. Even during the eight years of the Eisenhower presidency, the Democratic majority in Congress often set the agenda for domestic policies.[4] "Should any political party attempt to abolish Social Security, unemployment insurance and eliminate labor laws and farm programs," wrote Dwight Eisenhower in 1954, "you would not hear again of that political party in our political history."[5] Indeed, the crushing defeat of Republican Barry Goldwater in the 1964 presidential election was a reminder of

2. In 1956, 20 percent of those polled were independents. By 1989 the percentages had changed to Democrat 38 percent, Republican 34 percent and independent 28 percent. See James Ceasar, "Political Parties—Declining, Stabilizing or Resurging?" in Anthony King, ed., *The New American Political System*, (2d version) (Washington, D.C.: AEI Press, 1990). pp. 87–137.

3. See Theodore Lowi, *The End of Liberalism: The Second Republic of the United States*, 2d ed. (New York: Norton, 1979), pp. 273–74, for a discussion of the impact of the New Deal on the coming of the "Second Republic."

4. V. O. Key, *Politics, Parties, and Pressure Groups*, 4th ed. (New York: Crowell, 1958), p. 205. James Sundquist concluded that during the Eisenhower years the modern notion of president-congressional relations was reversed; the initiative for most policy measures belonged to the Democratically controlled Congress. See James Sundquist, *Politics and Policy: The Eisenhower, Kennedy, and Johnson Years* (Washington, D.C.: Brookings Institution, 1968).

5. Quoted in Michael Barone, *Our Country: The Shaping of America from Roosevelt to Reagan* (New York: Free Press, 1990), p. 279.

the fate of those who challenged the wisdom of Eisenhower's assessment. Held together by the harrowing memories of the Great Depression, a shared faith in the redemptive powers of a powerful national government led by an activist president and a steady stream of programs and benefits flowing from Washington, the coalition of minorities forged by Roosevelt—unionized labor, Catholic ethnics, Jews, public-sector employees, white southerners, and northern blacks—proved to be a remarkably stable and powerful governing regime in post–World War II America.

Although the New Deal would have a profound impact on the constitutional jurisprudence of the twentieth century, the politics of judicial confirmations during this period, notwithstanding Roosevelt's famous Court-packing plan of 1937, were actually rather uneventful. Roosevelt may have lost the Court-packing battle—the plan was never enacted—but he did ultimately win the war. In the spring of 1937 the Court reversed positions, upholding a state minimum-wage law and validating several key New Deal measures, including the National Labor Relations Act and the Social Security Act of 1935.[6] The Court's famous "switch in time that saved nine" coupled with the long-anticipated retirement of recalcitrant justices defused the conflict and shifted the focus of New Dealers—and their opponents—from the staffing of the Supreme Court to the building of a powerful administrative state.

Between 1937 and 1943, for example, Roosevelt named eight justices to the Supreme Court and elevated Harlan Fiske Stone to the chief justiceship. In retrospect, what is particularly remarkable about Roosevelt's new Court is the ease—especially in light of the brouhaha over the Court-packing plan—with which several contro-

6. *West Coast Hotel* v. *Parrish*, 300 U.S. 379 (1937) (sustaining a Washington state minimum-wage law); *NLRB* v. *Jones and Laughlin Steel Corp.*, 301 U.S. 1 (1937) (upholding the National Labor Relations Act); *Stewart Machine Company* v. *Davis*, 301 U.S. 548 (1937) (upholding the unemployment excise tax provisions of the Social Security Act); *Helvering* v. *Davis*, 301 U.S. 619 (1937) (upholding the old-age tax and benefits provision of the Social Security Act). For a highly readable account of the Supreme Court and the emerging welfare state of the New Deal, see Robert McCloskey, *The American Supreme Court* (Chicago: Univ. of Chicago Press, 1960), esp. chap. 6.

versial figures were placed on the Court. Felix Frankfurter, for instance, was America's most famous law professor, a founder of the
American Civil Liberties Union, defender of Sacco and Vanzetti, and
a close, as well as controversial, adviser to Roosevelt.[7] His "paper
trail" was far longer and his politics more controversial than Robert
Bork's were fifty years later. Hugo Black was a contentious New Deal
senator from Alabama and a former member of the Ku Klux Klan.
William Douglas, as chairman of the Securities and Exchange Commission, had made few friends in the financial community and was
characterized as a "radical" by the *New York Times.* Wiley Rutledge,
while dean of the Iowa University School of Law, had so infuriated
Iowa legislators with his support of the Roosevelt Court-packing plan
that they had threatened to withhold university salary increases.

Each nomination gained the advice and consent of the Senate
handily. Roosevelt anticipated opposition only with the Frankfurter
appointment, but, aside from some allegations that Frankfurter was a
Communist, the appointment passed the Senate easily. During this era
of its dominance, the Democratic party concentrated on linking its
diverse components through patronage, compromise, and vote trading. Ideological conflict was submerged beneath a pragmatic concern
with the distribution of goods and services. The coalition could ill
afford protracted battles over judicial appointments, and, thanks to
the expansion of the administrative branch and the Supreme Court's
retreat from economic policy-making, such battles were largely unnecessary.

7. Sacco and Vanzetti were Italian immigrants charged with the murder of a
paymaster and a guard in Braintree, Massachusetts, in 1920. Coming at the height of the
Red scare following World War I, the trial saw the prosecution play to the jury's bias
against immigrants and fear of political radicalism (the defendants were both admitted
anarchists and draft evaders). Both men were convicted and sentenced to death despite
substantial evidence of their innocence, and the case became a cause célèbre among
American intellectuals and progressives. Frankfurter wrote a scathing analysis of the case
in the *Atlantic Monthly,* documenting the legal errors and prejudice that produced the
guilty verdicts. The article galvanized supporters of the two men to continue to fight to
keep Sacco and Vanzetti alive. The article also enraged conservatives and produced in
many a lifelong hatred for Frankfurter. Despite the efforts of Frankfurter and others, the
men were eventually executed.

Roosevelt's death, in 1945, brought Harry Truman to the White House, and, although his four appointments to the Court were mediocre by any measure, they too elicited little opposition. Even the Republican capture of the presidency in 1952 scarcely ruffled the apparent calm that marked judicial confirmations of the era. The moderate Eisenhower administration coexisted quite well with the Democratic Congress, and Eisenhower made no effort to use his personal popularity to spearhead a Republican challenge to Democratic hegemony. Even when he was confronted by a Democratic Congress, his appointments to the Court secured confirmation by wide margins. The courts of this era constituted a primary concern only when they thwarted the policy goals of the New Deal coalition, and after 1937 the federal judiciary studiously avoided intervention in the policy areas closest to the heart of the governing regime.

The Pervasive Problem of Race

Hence one explanation for the lack of conflict over nominations to the Court in the years following the New Deal lies in the relative strength of the Democratic governing coalition. The slow dissolution of this coalition, however, is a basic plot line in the saga of American politics over the last three decades. Again 1968 is a pivotal year. In the presidential election Richard Nixon and independent candidate George Wallace combined for 57 percent of the vote and dealt a devastating defeat to the Democratic party and its candidate, Hubert Humphrey. The capacity of the Wallace candidacy to attract almost ten million votes, a substantial number from traditional white Democratic voters, was a harbinger of the fate that awaited future Democratic candidates for national office. During the early 1960s a substantial black vote had become requisite to Democratic success in presidential elections, and the party responded by trying to weld black voters to the party through the promotion of civil rights legislation. The strategy proved strikingly successful, and blacks formed a solidly Democratic bloc of voters. Today, although blacks make up only about 11 percent of the electorate, they provide approximately 20 percent of the Democratic vote in national elections.[8]

The backlash triggered by this strategy among white voters, however, has been a defining characteristic of modern American politics.[9] In 1952 some 70 percent of all white southerners considered themselves Democrats; during the next thirty years that percentage was cut in half. In 1980 and 1984 southern whites gave Ronald Reagan solid majorities and in 1988 preferred Bush to Dukakis by a margin of almost two to one. White southerners, an important component of the New Deal coalition, provided the bedrock of support for George Wallace in 1968. The Wallace campaign, in effect, provided a way station for white southern voters making the ideological journey from "the party of their fathers" to the new Republican majority, in response to what political scientist Robert Weissberg has termed "the blackening of the Democratic party."[10]

The migration of the civil rights movement during the 1960s from the rural South to the urban North intensified the exodus of whites from the Democratic party. The ethnic voter who populated America's northern and midwestern industrial cities was another important ingredient in Roosevelt's Democratic party. From the years of the New Deal through 1960, approximately one-third of the Democratic votes came from white union members and their families. Between 1964 and 1988 this base of support steadily eroded; in the

8. From 1948 through 1960, blacks constituted, at the most, one in twelve Democratic votes. In 1988 almost one in five Dukakis voters was black. See Paul Abramson et al., *Change and Continuity in the 1988 Elections* (Washington, D.C.: CQ Press, 1990), p. 135.

9. See Thomas Edsall and Mary Edsall, *Chain Reaction: The Impact of Race, Rights, and Taxes on American Politics* (New York: Norton, 1991). For a similar view of the impact of race on the New Deal coalition, see Benjamin Ginsberg and Martin Shefter, *Politics by Other Means: The Declining Importance of Elections in America* (New York: Basic, 1990). Whether the election of Bill Clinton in 1992 marks the arrival of a "new" Democratic party and coalition, or merely a momentary return of white "Reagan-Democrats" to the fold, remains to be seen.

10. Robert Weissberg, "The Democratic Party and the Conflict over Racial Policy," in Benjamin Ginsberg and Alan Stone, eds., *Do Elections Matter?* (Armonk, N.Y.: Sharpe, 1986).

1988 election only one in five Democratic votes came from white union members. The significance of this development can be further illustrated from the perspective of class, irrespective of union membership. In 1948 almost 50 percent of the Democratic vote came from working-class whites; in 1988 only 28 percent of the vote did.[11] Democratic voting among white Catholics has shown a similar long-term decline. Increasingly urban ethnics came to identify the Democratic party with the redistribution of benefits to black interests. By the late 1980s academic studies had confirmed what many observers of American politics had long suspected: among voters attitudes regarding race had become a critical variable in determining party identification.[12]

Racial antagonism, of course, is not the only explanation for the decline in the Democratic vote during the last three decades. Broad social and economic changes combined with shifts in the political environment to take a heavy toll on the New Deal coalition. Union membership in the United States has declined markedly, and the income distinctions between working and middle class have blurred. Because most voters now identify with a broad, well-to-do middle class, the traditional Democratic appeal to working-class interests apparently falls on deaf ears. Memories of Roosevelt and the New Deal link fewer voters to the Democratic party; by the late 1960s younger voters, lacking a personal connection to the Democrats, began to replace the generation of voters emotionally wedded to the party of Franklin Roosevelt. To the older generation the New Deal

11. Abramson et al., *Change and Continuity*, pp. 139, 141.
12. Edward G. Carmines and James A. Stimson, *Issue Evolution: Race and the Transformation of American Politics* (Princeton: Princeton Univ. Press, 1989); Robert R. Huckfeldt and Carol Kohfeld, *Race and the Decline of Class in American Politics* (Urbana: Univ. of Illinois Press, 1989). So important is this development to Republican success at the national level that the task for Republican presidential candidates is how to make the appropriate appeal without opening themselves to charges of overt racism. I will argue in the following chapter that, beginning with Richard Nixon in 1968, appeals and promises regarding the staffing of the federal courts in general and the Supreme Court specifically have provided Republican candidates with a convenient vehicle for delivering the racial message without breaching "political" good taste.

was a defining political event; the label "New Dealer" or "Anti–New Dealer" signified one's position across a broad range of political, social, and economic issues.[13] To the new generation of voters, the New Deal is merely a term encountered in history books. Generational change coupled with broad alterations in the political landscape, including the demise of patronage and the advent of television, had by 1968 clearly taken their toll on the national Democratic party.

The New Progressives

Roosevelt's political genius found expression in forging a majority coalition out of competing minority interests. By the late 1960s, however, the coalition was in disarray. In the aftermath of the 1968 election debacle, a battle for the heart (and mind) of the party developed between the traditional New Deal Democrats with roots in the union halls and Democratic clubs and a new generation "who had earned their political spurs in the civil rights movement and later in the antiwar movement" and who sought to refocus the party's priorities to fit the needs of an expanding suburban middle class.[14] The violence of the Chicago national convention and the results of the 1968 election hastened a movement to "democratize" the party's candidate selection procedures, by broadening the groups and opinions represented in the process. A not unanticipated result of this effort was to diminish the power of old-line party regulars. The new guidelines for delegate selection adopted before the 1972 convention changed the demographics at the convention—the proportion of blacks, youth, and women dramatically increased—and showcased the emergence of a new and powerful force in the party. The appear-

13. "The point about the ideas of the New Deal was not that they constituted a source of political division in America, but that for more than thirty years they constituted *the* source of political division" (emphasis in original). Anthony King, "The American Polity in the Late 1970s: Building Coalitions in the Sand," in Anthony King, ed., *The New American Political System* (Washington, D.C.: AEI Press, 1978), p. 372.

14. Thomas Byrne Edsall, *The New Politics of Inequality* (New York: Norton, 1984), p. 49.

ance of what I term the New Progressives not only transformed the nature of the Democratic party but also had a profound, albeit unexpected, impact on the politics of judicial selection.[15]

In her important study of the delegates to the 1972 political conventions, Professor Jeane Kirkpatrick wrote of the emergence of a new "presidential elite," political activists with higher income, higher education, higher social status, and less religious commitment than both party voters and old-line party activists.[16] At the 1972 Democratic National Convention, over 80 percent of the delegates had never attended a previous convention; approximately one-third had less than five years' experience in politics. By income, occupation, and status, the new delegates formed a representative sample not of the American electorate but of America's skilled professionals.[17] The ascendancy of the New Progressives, Professor Kirkpatrick predicted, would alter our understanding of Democratic party politics:

> Politics conducted by . . . [this group] will probably feature more emphasis on the symbolic aspects of politics and less on the output

15. Although social scientists have acknowledged the existence of this new "elite," there has been little agreement on precisely what to call it. Neoconservatives have written of a new class. See B. Bruce-Briggs, ed., *The New Class?* (New Brunswick, N.J.: Transaction, 1979). And political scientists Benjamin Ginsberg and Martin Shefter used the phrase "New Politics Movement." See their "A Critical Realignment? The New Politics, the Reconstituted Right and the 1984 Election," in Michael Nelson, ed., *The Elections of 1984* (Washington, D.C.: CQ Press, 1985). Neither "class" nor "movement" seems quite right, and I will use "New Progressives" because, as upper-middle-class, educated, cosmopolitan professionals dedicated to good government and reform, this group broadly resembles the Progressives of the early twentieth century. The similarities are not exact but close enough to justify the title.

16. Jeane Kirkpatrick, *The New Presidential Elite* (New York: Russell Sage Foundation, 1976).

17. At the 1972 Democratic convention the characteristics defining the New Progressives were most prevalent among the supporters of George McGovern. For example, forty percent of the female and 49 percent of the male McGovern delegates held professional jobs or were highly qualified technical experts. Among the delegates of McGovern's chief rival for the nomination, Hubert Humphrey, the percentages were 31 percent and 42 percent. Some 43 percent of the male McGovern delegates had graduate degrees, while only 22 percent of the male Humphrey delegates had achieved similar academic status. Ibid, pp. 385–86.

of goods and services. . . . Politics dominated by [such] professionals is likely to have a higher ideological content and the political process is more likely to be conceived as an arena for setting public agendas and resolving more problems than as an arena for winning and compromising material interests.[18]

Throughout the 1960s and 1970s the issue that had galvanized the New Deal coalition—the scope and nature of the American welfare state—receded in significance and a cluster of new problems keyed to race, crime, and the Vietnam War created deep divisions in what remained of the old coalition. On many of these social and cultural issues, the New Progressives held positions more liberal than those of old-line Democratic delegates and considerably more liberal than those of the Democratic electorate.[19] Furthermore, the New Progressives gave party unity and cohesion a low priority. In the view of these activists, one did not support a candidate simply out of party loyalty or the pragmatic need to win elections; on the contrary, political activity was inextricably linked to policy preferences and ideological goals. The coming of age of the New Progressives markedly increased divisive disputes within the party; compromise, in the end, is more difficult when principle rather than patronage must be accommodated.

The nomination of George McGovern as the party's standard-bearer in the 1972 campaign marked a dramatic change in the Demo-

18. Ibid., pp. 71–72.
19. For example, on the issue of the balance between protecting the rights of the accused and fighting crime, 95 percent of the McGovern delegates generally favored the rights of the accused, compared with 78 percent of all the delegates to the 1972 Democratic convention. Only 36 percent of rank-and-file Democrats, however, favored the rights of the accused. By way of comparison, 21 percent of the delegates at the Republican convention chose the rights of the accused. Similar findings on issues like attitudes toward the military and political demonstrations led Professor Kirkpatrick to conclude that the policy preferences of the typical rank-and-file Democrat actually were closer to those of the delegates at the Republican convention than to those of the delegates at the Democratic convention. While delegates to national conventions are traditionally more politicized than the average Republican or Democratic, the distinctions found by Kirkpatrick between Democratic delegates and identifiers were noteworthy, and the distinctions between the rank and file and McGovern delegates were extraordinary. Ibid., chap. 10.

cratic party, and, despite his decisive defeat at the hands of Richard Nixon, McGovern remains an important figure in modern American history. His nomination testified to the capacity of the New Progressives to challenge the party bosses; no longer a small, isolated fringe group contesting American involvement in Southeast Asia, McGovern and his supporters quickly became a dominant force in the party. The reform of the nominating procedures adopted by the Democrats in the early 1970s gave life to the McGovern candidacy and continues to this day to skew the process in favor of the New Progressives, despite the persistent efforts of the old guard to redress the balance.[20] Furthermore, the McGovern campaign accentuated the redirection of the party's primary focus from the urban blue-collar worker, who formed the backbone of support for Roosevelt and Truman, to the professional living in America's expanding suburbs.[21]

The McGovern campaign of 1972 may have heralded a new force in the Democratic party, but the cruel reality of the Nixon landslide in the general election showcased the insurgents' failure to appeal to a broad, national electorate. The liberalism of the New Progressive was built upon a tolerance for changing social values and

20. The ebb and flow of reform in both parties is discussed in William Crotty, *Party Reform* (New York: Longman, 1983).

21. In the 1974 elections voter disgust with Watergate produced a crop of new legislators, reflecting the background and outlook of the New Progressives. There were ninety-two freshman representatives in what became known as "the class of '74," seventy-five were Democrats (and two-thirds of the newly elected Democrats were from districts previously represented by Republicans). For the majority of the class of '74, the civil rights movement and opposition to the Vietnam War were the defining events of their political lives, and the 1972 McGovern campaign constituted their introduction to organized Decmoratic politics. A fair number were political or social activists prior to their election. Upon their arrival in Congress in 1974, the new Democrats worked to limit the power of the party leadership and reform the committee system. Whereas the traditional Democratic leadership often reflected either the Old South or big-city politics, the class of '74 had a more polished suburban image, often mixing moderate economics with social liberalism. One skill shared by almost all the newcomers was an appreciation of the power of the media in modern American politics. The Democratic class of '74 continues to be a major power on Capitol Hill. See John Yang, "How the Watergate Class of '74 Played Kings of the Hill," *Washington Post National Weekly Edition*, June 22–28, 1992, p. 12. See also Hedrick Smith, *The Power Game: How Washington Works* (New York: Ballantine, 1989), for an extended discussion of "the new breed" of legislator.

lifestyles and was preoccupied with curtailing American intervention abroad while ignoring, for the most part, the bread-and-butter economic concerns that united the New Deal with working-class America. This crisis of Democratic party identification, made so manifest in the 1972 campaign, continued to haunt the party for the next two decades: although the tone and direction of the party remained with the New Progressives, electoral success every four years depended on a large voter turnout among more socially conservative, lower-income voters. In effect, from 1968 through the election of Bill Clinton in 1992, the Democratic party was a political party at war with itself.[22]

THE NEW PROGRESSIVES AND THE JUDICIARY

Electoral Defeats, Litigation Victories

Whether Bill Clinton's 1992 victory actually heralds the coming of a "new" Democratic party awaits the judgment of history. What is certain is that the period from the 1968 campaign through the Reagan-Bush era witnessed the unraveling of the old Democratic coalition. The disorder in the party produced among other things a new attention to the staffing of the federal judiciary. Repeated Democratic losses in presidential campaigns combined with the party's domination of Congress produced a presidential-legislative gridlock that made control of the third branch more important. The disdain of the New Progressives for the politics of patronage and vote trading led to congressional reforms that curtailed the ability of the leadership to cut the deals that formed the lifeblood of the old coalition, and the courts became a viable alternative forum for advancing segments of a progressive policy agenda. As the behind-the-scenes power of the leadership diminished, the likelihood of polarizing public battles over

22. For a brilliant analysis of the confusion of ideology in both the Democratic and Republican parties, see E. J. Dionne, Jr., *Why Americans Hate Politics* (New York: Simon & Schuster, 1991).

nominations to the federal courts naturally increased. But neither divided government nor a change in politics as usual adequately accounts for the highly divisive and bellicose politics of modern judicial confirmations.

In spite of their drubbings in national elections, the New Progressives have proven remarkably adept at securing many of their policy goals. To an extraordinary degree, the judiciary has been the institution responsible for these successes, in effect permitting the New Progressives to substitute court victories for electoral failures. For example, during the Nixon years the progressive wing of the Democratic party employed the judiciary to frustrate the expansion of executive power, establishing significant legal precedents limiting the authority of the executive to impound funds, to engage in domestic surveillance, and to halt the desegregation of the South. The Supreme Court's opinion in the Watergate tapes case was the coup de grace to the Nixon presidency.[23] Following the resignation of Nixon the New Progressive continued to use the federal courts to advance policy preferences ranging from safer working conditions to containment of the nuclear power industry. By the early 1970s the judiciary had become the institutional ally of an important segment of the Democratic party; as a result, appointments to the federal bench quickly evolved from being matters of political patronage to being decisions fraught with significant political consequences.

The crusade against pervasive and long-standing gender discrimination serves as an illuminating example of the New Progressives' heightened reliance on the federal courts to counter defeats in the electoral arena. Gender equality was (and continues to be) a central, defining policy goal of these activists, and the defeat of the Equal Rights Amendment (ERA) in 1982 dealt a bitter blow to forces aligned with the New Progressives. The failure of the ERA in the democratic process, however, was offset at least partly by the Supreme Court, the national institution that evidenced the greatest

---

23. See, generally, Mark Silverstein and Benjamin Ginsberg, "The Supreme Court and the New Politics of Judicial Power," *Political Science Quarterly* 102 (1987): 371.

commitment to gender equality during the 1970s and 1980s. In a 1973 case four justices reached the conclusion that gender, like race, was a "suspect classification" triggering the strictest level of judicial scrutiny. Had an additional justice voted to support this position, the New Progressives would have been spared the agony of the ERA defeat; in subjecting claims of gender discrimination to strict judicial scrutiny, the Court, in effect, would have judicially enacted the ERA ten years before its eventual defeat in the political arena.[24]

Notwithstanding the Court's ultimate refusal to treat gender discrimination as the legal equivalent of discrimination on the basis of race, a solid majority of the Court has continued to agree that claims of gender inequality should be judged by a heightened standard of review and, during the 1970s and 1980s, invalidated a broad assortment of statutes that drew distinctions on the basis of gender.[25] The federal judiciary has also proven quite willing to interpret federal statutes to further the goal of gender equality, particularly when the alleged discrimination strikes directly at matters of the most immediate professional concern to the New Progressives. In 1984, for example, the Court extended the federal law barring discrimination in the workplace to forbid sexual discrimination in a law firm's decision on whether to promote a female associate to the position of partner.[26]

Thanks to the active intervention of the federal courts, the New Progressives, despite the defeat of the ERA, were remarkably success-

24. *Frontiero* v. *Richardson,* 411 U.S. 67 (1973). The fifth judicial vote to make gender a suspect classification has not been forthcoming, and gender discrimination is reviewed under a judicial standard more lenient than that for racial discrimination. But consider the following note and the accompanying text.

25. For the last twenty years the Court has required the government to show that a challenged gender classification bears a close and substantial relationship to important governmental objectives. See *Craig* v. *Boren,* 429 U.S. 190 (1976). One measure of the potency of this standard of review was the Reagan administration's determined efforts to compel the Court to accept a more deferential standard. See *Mississippi University for Women* v. *Hogan,* 458 U.S. 718 (1982), a 5-to-4 decision upholding heightened scrutiny for claims of gender discrimination.

26. *Hishon* v. *King & Spaulding,* 467 U.S. 69 (1984). Consider also *Meritor Savings Bank* v. *Vinson,* 477 U.S. 57 (1986), concluding that sexual harassment in the workplace is actionable under Title VII of the Civil Rights Act of 1964.

ful in the war against sex discrimination. Indeed, by the 1970s the federal courts were often the arena most receptive to the policy goals of the New Progressives across a wide range of issues, and even the election of Democrat Jimmy Carter did little to counter this development. Carter was unable to reunite the old coalition, and therefore, throughout his administration, the factions in the Democratic party pursued their own agendas by whatever means and in whichever forums best served their interests. The fact that Democrats controlled both Congress and the executive had little impact; by the mid-1970s the Democratic party was so divided that the strategy and behavior of its disparate parts were only marginally altered by Democratic control of the White House.[27]

As a consequence, the New Progressives' attention to the staffing of the federal courts increased rather than decreased during the Carter years. For decades the civil rights establishment had carefully scrutinized judicial nominees, with varying impact on the process. With the coming of the Carter administration, both the degree of scrutiny and the number and political influence of the groups engaged in the endeavor increased materially. Groups with a professional, upper-middle-class focus such as the Women's Legal Defense Fund, the Center for Law and Social Policy, Common Cause, and the National Organization of Women began regularly to set aside funds and staff for the express purpose of keeping watch on nominees to the

27. E. J. Dionne describes the Carter presidency in this way: "His administration became a battleground in which all the tendencies of the Democratic Party, and all of the wings of liberalism, struggled for influence. Carter's appointees to regulatory commissions tended to be younger liberals much influenced by Ralph Nader–style public advocacy. Thus, on issues such as occupational health and safety, the environment, and consumer protection, the Carter administration had a decidedly progressive tinge. Carter himself was not always comfortable with this, commenting once that he was the most conservative member of his own administration. . . . On the social issues, the contradictions were between Carter's conservative personal behavior and his deep and genuine religious feeling, which had made him so attractive to Southern conservatives in his election campaign, and his relatively liberal views on issues relating to civil rights, women's rights, and civil liberties. . . . Social liberals mistrusted Carter's religiosity and his 'Southernness,' sensing that he did not fully share their cosmopolitan worldview. Social conservatives, in the meantime, saw Carter as betraying them." Dionne, *Why Americans Hate Politics*, p. 134.

federal bench. Through sympathetic advocates on the Senate Judiciary Committee (chaired then by Senator Edward Kennedy), these groups were in a position to ensure that nominees were often quizzed on matters of particular concern to the New Progressives, including support for affirmative action and the Equal Rights Amendment.[28] With Jimmy Carter in the White House, the New Progressives' efforts to promote the consideration of judicial "activists" as well as "nontraditional" nominees (that is, people of color and women) to the federal bench were enormously successful. Although denied an opportunity to nominate a Supreme Court justice, Carter appointed more women and minority judges than had all previous presidents combined.[29]

THE NEW PROGRESSIVES IN THE REPUBLICAN ERA

The Reagan Years

The 1980 victory of Ronald Reagan and the Democratic loss of the Senate for the first time in twenty-eight years drove the final nails into the coffin of the New Deal coalition. Reagan drew substantial support from white southerners, blue-collar workers, and Catholics, while many Democratic progressives rejected Carter for the independent

28. In 1977 President Carter announced the creation of the Circuit Court Nominating Commission. The commission was divided into panels, one for each judicial circuit, and was charged with recruiting and screening candidates for vacancies on the courts of appeals and submitting a recommendation to the president. The idea behind the commission was to remove the more blatant aspects of political patronage from the judicial selection process. In practice, however, the panels of the commission provided New Progressives with an additional forum to screen candidates for judicial appointments. See Larry C. Berkson et al., "A Study of the U.S. Circuit Judge Nominating Commission: Findings, Conclusions and Recommendations," *Judicature* 63 (1980): 105; Elliot E. Slotnick, "The Changing Role of the Senate Judiciary Committee in Judicial Selection," *Judicature* 62 (1979): 502. One of the first actions of the Reagan administration was to discontinue the nominating commission.

29. Carter appointed twenty-eight African-Americans, twenty-nine women (including six African-American women), and fourteen Hispanics. Carter's appointments alone increased the percentage of women on the federal bench from 1 percent to 7 percent. See Sheldon Goldman, "Carter's Judicial Appointments: A Lasting Legacy," *Judicature* 64 (1981): 344.

candidacy of Republican liberal John Anderson.[30] Once in office, Reagan inspired tax and spending policies that further interred any hopes of resurrecting Democratic hegemony. A substantial reduction in the top federal income tax rates linked many of the newly affluent to the Republican party, while the deep cuts in government revenue diminished the distributive capacity of the national government and the Democrats' ability to disburse the goods and services necessary to the maintenance of the old coalition. Republican dominance of the executive branch heightened the intensity of conflict among factions in the Democratic party, as increasing budget deficits and decreasing revenues forced the beneficiaries of federal programs to fight for a smaller piece of an ever-diminishing pie.[31]

The coming of the Reagan presidency made the staffing of the federal judiciary even more important to the New Progressives and focused much of their political energy. The loss of the Senate in 1980 left liberals off balance, and the initial Reagan appointments to the lower federal courts produced limited conflict. The burden of investigating these initial nominees fell to the civil rights establishment, led by the Leadership Conference on Civil Rights.[32] By 1984, however, groups broadly associated with the New Progressives had identified the federal courts as essential points of conflict and organized the Judicial Selection Project to coordinate efforts in the battle against

30. Although Reagan essentially split the blue-collar vote with Carter in 1980, this was a substantial improvement over Gerald Ford's showing with these voters in 1976. In 1984 Reagan garnered 53 percent of the blue-collar vote. In short, from 1976 to 1984 the Republican share of blue-collar voters increased by approximately 12 percent. In the case of white southerners, the increase from 1976 to 1984 was nearly twenty percent. A substantial portion of Anderson's support came from upper-income, college-educated voters. See Gerald M. Pomper, *The Election of 1984: Reports and Interpretations* (Chatham, N.J.: Chatham House, 1985), pp. 67–69.

31. See, for example, Ginsberg and Shefter, *Politics by Other Means*, pp. 102–8.

32. The LCCR was established by the NAACP in 1950 to coordinate lobbying campaigns on behalf of civil rights measures and quickly emerged as the preeminent coalition of civil rights organizations in the country. Its longtime general counsel was Joseph Rauh, who, until his death in 1992, was one of the giants of the civil rights movement in the United States, and its executive director, Ralph Neas, is generally acknowledged to be one of the most sophisticated students of the legislative process in Washington, D.C.

Reagan's judicial appointments. Counting among its members progressive interests as diverse as the Women's Legal Defense and Education Fund, Consumers Union, the National Wildlife Federation, the Children's Defense Fund, the National Education Association, and People for the American Way, the Judicial Selection Project joined with the LCCR to scrutinize nominees to the federal bench, investigating their records, organizing grassroots opposition, and maintaining important links to key Democrats on the Senate Judiciary Committee.[33] In 1986 the citizens' group Common Cause joined the effort, publishing a report that admonished the Senate Judiciary Committee, in the name of responsible, democratic government, to examine with great care the Reagan nominees to the federal judiciary.

That same year the efforts of the progressive interests to direct liberal attention to the staffing of the federal courts gained momentum when Reagan nominated Daniel Manion of Indiana to the Seventh Circuit Court of Appeals. A strident conservative with the slimmest of professional qualifications, Manion enraged liberals with his links to the John Birch Society and his abiding faith that the Constitution permitted the posting of the Ten Commandments in the nation's classrooms. New Progressives united with traditional civil rights groups to form a potent opposition to the Manion nomination. For example, funds for full-page ads in national newspapers and television spots opposing the nomination were provided by People for the American Way, a well-financed New Progressive organization founded by television producer Norman Lear in 1981 to counteract

33. The project was established under the auspices of the Alliance for Justice, a coalition of approximately twenty public-interest groups formed in the early 1980s to facilitate lobbying and organizing efforts on behalf of progressive concerns. Although the NAACP and the LCCR were included in the Judicial Selection Project, a tension quickly developed between the old-line civil rights organizations and several of the New Progressive groups associated with the Alliance for Justice. Many traditional civil rights organizations, often with links to church groups like the Catholic Conference, were anti-abortion, while reproductive choice was a paramount concern of many important New Progressive groups like NARAL and Planned Parenthood and a goal generally supported by almost all professional, upper-middle-class interests. This tension surfaced during the organization phase of the battle against the nomination of Robert Bork. See Mark Gitenstein, *Matters of Principle* (New York: Simon & Schuster, 1992), p. 170ff.

the influence of the religious Right. Although Manion was ultimately confirmed by the Senate, thanks to the tie-breaking vote of Vice-President George Bush, the surprisingly effective and well-financed battle against the nomination displayed the political strength and skills that New Progressives could bring to the contesting of judicial nominations.[34]

For decades civil rights groups monitored judicial appointments. They tended to exercise their, at times considerable influence quietly, relying on carefully cultivated contacts with senators and staff, developed through years of playing the Washington power game. The impact of the New Progressives, however, on the traditional, insider politics of judicial selection was electrifying. Substantial resources and a keenly developed appreciation of media politics all but transformed the old system. During the Manion confirmation fight, for example, Senator Slade Gorton, Republican of Washington, was battling for his political life in a tough campaign for reelection. Gorton struck a deal with the Reagan administration, agreeing to vote for Manion's confirmation in return for the administration's support of Gorton's nominee to the federal bench in the state of Washington. Throughout the history of the Republic, similar deals had been made thousands of times without any attendant publicity or adverse electoral consequence. The reality of the modern politics of judicial confirmations, however, is that what was once mundane is now remarkable. Gorton's Democratic opponent seized on the deal to support Manion, and it quickly became an important factor in the defeat of an incumbent senator.[35] That a senator from the state of Washington might be held accountable for a vote to approve an appointment to a midwestern federal judgeship was a startling development that caught the collec-

34. For a description of the tactics and strategy of the groups opposing Manion, see Philip Shenon, "Praise and Pillory for a Liberal Lobby Group," *New York Times,* Aug. 6, 1986, pp. A1, A16.

35. For a description of the reaction of Washington voters and newspapers to the Manion vote, see Bill Prochnau, "Vote Swap Blows Up in Senator Gorton's Face; Deal on Judgeships Is Political Dynamite in Washington State," *Washington Post,* July 11, 1986, p. A1.

tive attention of Gorton's Senate colleagues.[36] In the aftermath of the Manion battle, few senators would disagree with Ann Lewis, the director of the Americans for Democratic Action, when she observed that a "senator's actions on judges is [sic] becoming a salient issue" to many important interests.[37]

By the end of Reagan's first term, the New Deal coalition lay in the distant political past. The various factions in the Democratic party had adapted their goals and methods to the reality of Republican domination of the executive branch. The New Progressives made an activist judiciary an indispensable ally in formulating and securing their policy agenda. The linkage between the federal courts and politically potent middle- and upper-middle-class interests is a very significant development in modern American politics. It explains, for example, a good deal of the turmoil generated by Reagan's nomination of Robert Bork to the Supreme Court in 1986. From the perspective of the New Progressives, Bork was unacceptable on the Supreme Court because he was the most accomplished, forceful, and unrelenting critic of judicial activism of his generation. The defeat of his nomination therefore became a matter of overwhelming importance to liberal interests and demanded a strategy designed to highlight the potential impact of his narrow interpretation of the federal judicial role on the policy objectives of numerous New Progressive groups.

36. More recently, a Bush nomination of an Alabama prosecutor to the Eleventh Circuit Court of Appeals raised similar problems for Republican Arlen Specter of Pennsylvania. The nomination of Edward Carnes, known for his skill and tenacity in arguing against death sentence appeals while an assistant attorney general in Alabama, triggered opposition by civil rights groups contending that in his zeal to defend executions Carnes was insensitive to racial issues. Democrats promised a filibuster, but a cloture motion succeeded and the Senate confirmed Carnes by a 62-to-36 margin. Senator Specter, a member of the Senate Judiciary Committee and engaged in a tough reelection battle, had voted for the confirmation of Carnes when his nomination was before the Judiciary Committee. His Democratic opponent in the Senate race in Pennsylvania made the nomination of Carnes an important campaign issue, and Specter switched positions and voted against the Carnes nomination when it reached the floor of the Senate. See Neil A. Lewis, "Court Nominee Is Confirmed after Angry Senate Debate," *New York Times*, Sept. 10, 1992, p. A16.

37. Quoted in Howard Kurtz, "Votes on Judge Nominees Become Politically Risky," *Washington Post*, June 28, 1986, p. A5.

The task was to frame the terms of the debate in a manner calculated to capture the attention of the myriad groups with a substantial stake in an activist judiciary without engaging in heavy-handed, extremist rhetoric certain to alienate many potential opponents of the nomination. To accomplish this difficult balancing act, activists opposing the Bork nomination relied upon the technology of modern electoral politics to find which of the issues associated with Bork resonated most powerfully among important interests. Polls and focus group studies, for example, showed a growing unease with Judge Bork's forceful critiques of the Supreme Court's guardianship of the unenumerated constitutional right to privacy. This right of privacy, first articulated by the Supreme Court in 1965 in *Griswold* v. *Connecticut*, became the constitutional linchpin for judicial protection of the abortion choice in *Roe* v. *Wade*.[38] Abortion, however, was a potentially divisive issue even among some New Progressives, while support of a protected right of privacy tapped into a widely shared belief among liberals and conservatives that government should not dictate personal lifestyle decisions. Because of polling data, opponents of Bork made *Griswold*, rather than the far more familiar (at least to the public at large), *Roe* a key "talking point" in the battle against Bork.[39] Modern technology gave Bork's opponents not simply data to convince senators of constituent opposition to the nomination but, even more important, the means to generate this opposition by linking the concerns of politically important groups to the Bork record.

In the end the Bork nomination was turned aside because the power and resources of numerous New Progressive groups combined with the efforts of the traditional civil rights community to form a potent political force. That over three hundred organizations, ranging from the National Black Leadership Roundtable to the Association of Flight Attendants and SANE/FREEZE, actively opposed Bork was

38. *Griswold* v. *Connecticut*, 381 U.S. 479 (1965); *Roe* v. *Wade*, 410 U.S. 113 (1973).
39. For a discussion on the evolution of privacy as a key element in the campaign to defeat Bork, see Michael Pertschuk and Wendy Schaetzel, *The People Rising* (New York: Thunder's Mouth Press, 1989), esp. chap. 6; Gitenstein, *Matters of Principle*, chap. 8.

due largely to the struggle of the LCCR and the Judicial Selection Project to turn the concerns of the New Progressives with the staffing of the federal judiciary into concrete political action. The prevalence of professional women's groups, for example, among the many interests opposing Bork testified to the power of the New Progressives and the significance in the 1980s of the judiciary to a new constituency beyond the civil rights community.

The National Federation of Business and Professional Women's Clubs is a case in point. The organization, which has many Republican members, concentrated in the South and Midwest, actively opposed the Bork nomination. "Here were all the issues we cared about embodied in one fight," explained Monica McFadden, the lobbyist for the association. "Senators know we're not nut cases. We're very moderate as a group. The average age of our members is late forties, early fifties."[40] That a moderately progressive organization could be energized by a campaign against a conservative Republican, nominee to the Supreme Court shows the salience of the Court appointments to a far wider range of interests than ever before in its institutional history.

A Kinder and Gentler Politics of Judicial Confirmations?

The coming of George Bush's "kinder and gentler" politics did not significantly alter the New Progressives' absorption with the shape of the federal judiciary. The failure of the 1988 Dukakis campaign and the stalemate produced by divided rule simply magnified the significance of control of the third branch. The threat to the continued vitality of *Roe* v. *Wade* and the constitutional protection of abortion rights riveted the New Progressives' attention on the judiciary and Bush appointments to the federal bench. Conservative groups were equally attentive to nominations to the federal bench (see chapter 4) and, in the wake of the Bork defeat, vowed that future conservative nominees would not suffer a similar fate. In the White House, strate-

---

40. Quoted in Ethan Bronner, *Battle for Justice* (New York: Norton, 1989), p. 186.

gists sought out nominees who could satisfy conservatives while presenting qualities that would undercut a hostile New Progressive—civil rights alliance.

These cross-pressures produced David Souter to replace the retiring Justice Brennan as the first Bush appointment to the Court. Souter had served as New Hampshire's attorney general and later as a state trial and appellate court judge before being appointed to the U.S. court of appeals a scant three months before his nomination to the high court. Most important, he had left almost no paper trail; he had published no scholarly articles, written no widely acclaimed books, and produced, as a state supreme court justice, no distinctive opinions that attracted the attention of legal commentators. He presented, in the words of Senator Paul Simon, "as blank a slate as anyone ever offered by a President for a seat on the Court."[41] Everyone was equally in the dark regarding Judge Souter. Liberals, however, were quietly assured by Senator Warren Rudman, the respected Republican of New Hampshire and a close friend of the nominee, that Souter was as good as they could possibly hope to get from the Bush administration. Conservatives eventually were forced to trust the promises of the president and the judgment of the Department of Justice. Armed with a quiet, restrained style and doggedly refusing to engage members of the Senate Judiciary Committee in a substantive discussion of his judicial philosophy, Souter (quickly dubbed the "stealth nominee") was easily confirmed.

Souter's nomination reflected the state of the modern process of judicial selection and appointment. In 1932 President Hoover had been compelled to bring Benjamin Cardozo to the Court because of his renown as a judicial scholar and state court jurist. Almost sixty years later there was not the slightest suggestion of an outpouring of professional demand for Judge Souter. No one seriously suggested that he was among the most prominent jurists in the land. Nor could the nominee lay claim to a long-standing friendship or professional

41. Paul Simon, *Advice and Consent* (Washington, D.C.: National Press Books, 1992), p. 76.

relationship with the president; indeed, we can be relatively certain that Bush knew little about the nominee in the days before his appointment was announced. Although Judge Souter had the important support of Senator Rudman and White House Chief of Staff John Sununu (the former governor of New Hampshire), the inescapable conclusion is that the White House selected Judge Souter precisely because he was an unknown.

One year later, when Thurgood Marshall announced his retirement from the Court, the Bush administration gambled on a different strategy to achieve the same goal: satisfying conservatives while choosing a nominee with qualities that would forestall significant opposition on the part of the New Progressive and the civil rights community. In the view of the Bush White House, Clarence Thomas fit the bill perfectly. Conservatives were elated. Unlike Justice Souter, Thomas was an avowed conservative, having written and spoken extensively in support of the Right's social agenda. And, despite President Bush's disingenuous claim that the Thomas appointment "has nothing to do with race," it was precisely race and the nominee's humble origins that the White House counted on to deter New Progressive hostility.

To quell liberal opposition, the White House and Thomas supporters offered poignant tales of Thomas's youth in the segregated, backwater town of Pin Point, Georgia, in an initially successful effort to have this rags-to-riches saga define his public persona. During the hearings before the Senate Judiciary Committee, the Pin Point strategy shielded him from a searching examination regarding his mediocre professional background and his limited and undistinguished record as a judge. Given Thomas's personal history, senators normally allied with the New Progressives found it difficult to probe and challenge either his extremely conservative judicial philosophy or his commitment to civil rights. New Progressives and senators alike were uneasy challenging the credentials of a nominee to the Supreme Court who could speak so movingly of surviving the indignities of apartheid in America. Although his slim professional record and conservative views assured a fair number of negative votes on the Senate floor,

Clarence Thomas was well on his way to confirmation until Anita Hill and allegations of sexual harassment appeared on the scene.

Bill Clinton and Beyond

The Bush nominees to the Court represent an important stage in the evolution of the modern process of judicial selection and confirmation. Prior to 1968 twentieth-century presidents could rest reasonably certain of a successful nomination to the Court. The process of selecting and confirming even a Supreme Court justice excited minimal public interest and, as long as the nominee had the basic legal and political qualifications, senators, regardless of party affiliation, could be expected to support the nominee. Today vacancies on the Supreme Court present the president with a daunting challenge. The constellation of political and legal forces at work in the nation virtually guarantees a potentially powerful *opposition* in response to any nomination, and thus the modern president is compelled to seek out nominees who present characteristics certain to forestall, or at least minimize, this opposition. That these qualities may have little to do with excellence on the bench is part of the reality of the modern process of judicial selection and confirmation.

The election of Democrat Bill Clinton in 1992 assures certain changes in the dynamics of judicial selection. With one of their own in the White House, New Progressives may well find unified government more to their liking and focus greater attention on legislative and executive policy-making, particularly if Clinton shows signs of leading a long-term Democratic revival. At the very least, New Progressives are certain to play a major role in finding friendly candidates for the federal judiciary and promoting their nomination to the new administration. The role, even if more pleasant and satisfying than that of the loyal opposition, may prove no less daunting. Waiting in the wings to scrutinize potential nominees and mobilize their supporters is a network of right-wing activists, equally appreciative of the increased importance of

the federal judiciary and well schooled in the strategy and tech-
niques of the modern politics of judicial confirmations. To complete the picture of how changes in electoral politics have influenced the selection of our judges, we must thus turn to the
other side of the aisle and consider developments within the Republican party.

Chapter 4

THE REPUBLICANS: THE COMING
OF THE NEW RIGHT

Judicial nominations have assumed greater import for elements in the Republican party as well. The Republican domination of national elections began in 1968, with Richard Nixon's successful bid for the presidency, and continued through the presidencies of Ronald Reagan and George Bush. For Nixon, campaigning against the alleged liberal excesses of the Warren Court emerged as a prime theme for linking middle America to the Republican party. In the 1980s the Republican coalition was anchored, on the one end, by upper-income Americans favored by Republican tax and economic policies and, on the other, by lower-income southern whites and northern ethnics attracted to the "family values" agenda emphasized by the modern Republican party. For Reagan and Bush, promises to employ the appointment power to alter the makeup of the Supreme Court to further a conservative social agenda allowed the Republican party to forge a strong link with the New Right while redirecting the attention of this important component of the Republican party away from the legislative agenda of the executive branch to the staffing of the federal courts.

THE RISE OF THE NEW REPUBLICAN MAJORITY

Running against the Court

On the eve of the 1968 Republican National Convention, Richard Nixon addressed several southern delegations. In Washington the Fortas nomination was in jeopardy, and Nixon was asked his thoughts on the appointment of a new chief justice. "I don't know what the Senate is going to do," Nixon stated,

> but if I have the chance to appoint Justices to the Supreme Court, they will be the kind of men I want—and I want men who are strict constructionalists, men that try to interpret the law and don't try to make the law. I want men, for example, who are for civil rights, but who recognize that the first civil right of every American is to be free from domestic violence. That is the kind of men we are going to have, and I think we need that kind of balance in the courts.

Later that week, during his acceptance speech, Nixon restated a theme he would repeat throughout his campaign: "Let us always respect, as I do, our courts and those who serve on them, but let us also recognize that some of our courts in their dissents [*sic*] have gone too far in weakening the police forces against the criminal forces of this country."[1] The Nixon campaign had begun in earnest.

The task for Nixon was to develop a winning coalition out of the ashes of Goldwater's crushing defeat in 1964. The key components would be southern white defectors from the Democratic party and their northern counterparts. Kevin Phillips, then a young Nixon strategist, captured the spirit of the enterprise: "Who needs Manhattan when we can get the electoral votes of eleven Southern states? Put those together with the Farm Belt and the Rocky Mountains and we don't need the cities. We don't even want them. Sure Hubert [Humphrey] will carry Riverside Drive [in New York City] in November. La-de-dah. What will he do in Oklahoma?"[2] Nixon's Republican revival would be fueled by a powerful lower-middle-class populism. Angered by rising crime rates and welfare rolls and threatened by cultural upheaval, the "silent majority" would become the new Republican majority. The 1968 Nixon campaign did not invoke the

1. Quoted in Bruce Murphy, *Fortas* (New York: Morrow, 1988), pp. 466–67.
2. Quoted in Gary Wills, *Nixon Agonistes: The Crisis of the Self-made Man* (New York: NAL, 1970), p. 248.

traditional Republican images of wealth and economic privilege; it did not speak the language of Palm Beach or even of Wall Street. Instead, the question asked about any campaign strategy was soon "How will it play in Peoria?"[3]

Whereas the liberal establishment was fair game and could be attacked directly—running mate Spiro Agnew's specialty—race was a more subtle and difficult card to play. George Wallace's third-party candidacy was also directed at middle America, and his appeal was more overtly racial. In the long term the Wallace campaign furthered Republican interests by dislodging Democrats from the party; in the short run, however, Wallace might attract many potential Nixon votes and throw the election to Humphrey.[4] The tightrope Nixon walked in 1968 demanded that he publicly support civil rights while simultaneously conveying sympathy and understanding for the "forgotten Americans" attracted to Wallace. The federal judiciary, and in particular the Supreme Court, provided a handy foil for making this appeal. Nixon's typical stump speech, echoing his acceptance speech in Miami, often began with a short, respectful testimonial to judges and equality under the law. Very quickly, however, he would castigate the Court for any one of many constitutional decisions that in his view weakened the police in the battle against crime or substituted a judge's social values for those of the people and their elected representatives.

The Court became the metaphor that allowed Nixon to play on

3. Or perhaps, better yet, "How will it play in Mobile?" The importance of the white South to Nixon is illustrated by the fact that in the thirty-nine states outside the South and the District of Columbia, Nixon lost to Humphrey by approximately 30,000 votes. In the eleven states of the South, Nixon led Humphrey by about 500,000 votes. William J. Keefe, *Parties, Politics and Public Policy in America* (New York: Holt, Rinehart and Winston, 1972), p. 34. Nixon received only 12 percent of the black vote, while 85 percent of the nonwhite voters cast their ballots for Hubert Humphrey.

4. While Nixon often contended that Wallace's appeal was racist, he was obsessed with the Wallace vote and the need to draw off a good deal of Wallace supporters if he was to win the election. One explanation for his choice of Spiro Agnew as running mate was Agnew's appeal to the Wallace constituency. See Stephen E. Ambrose, *Nixon: The Triumph of a Politician, 1962–1972* (New York: Simon & Schuster, 1989), pp. 163–65. Wallace ultimately won 9.9 million votes (13.5 percent) and 46 electoral votes. Nixon received 31.79 million votes (43.4 percent) and 301 electoral votes, to Humphrey's 31.25 million votes (42.7 percent) and 191 electoral votes.

racial divisions without violating the standards of civility demanded by mainstream American politics of the day. In a television broadcast shown in twelve southern and border states, Nixon attacked the Warren Court for constitutionalizing the "social ideas" of some of its members.[5] In the waning days of the campaign, Nixon assured voters that his judges would not be tempted to view themselves as "super-legislators with a free hand to impose their social and political viewpoints upon the American people."[6] Nixon responded to a late Humphrey surge by reminding voters that throughout the campaign his opponent had steadfastly refused to criticize the Court. "Whenever I begin to discuss the Supreme Court, Mr. Humphrey acts like we're in church. Mr. Humphrey's respectful silence [on controversial Court decisions] may stem from the fact that he has spent four years in [LBJ's] obedience school." Humphrey had done nothing, Nixon scornfully concluded, "while watching the United States become a nation where 50 percent of American women are frightened to walk within a mile of their homes at night."[7] In the supercharged atmosphere of the 1968 presidential campaign, silence on the subject of the Warren Court was not without political risk.

Richard Nixon: The Court as Scapegoat

The Nixon victory in 1968 began the Republican domination of the modern presidency. By eschewing the laissez-faire policies of earlier Republican administrations, Nixon hoped to transcend the image of the "party of privilege" and reinvent the Republican party as "the party of middle America." His economic program (particularly when contrasted with that of the Reagan and Bush presidencies) was pragmatic and evidenced a frankly New Deal faith in government intervention and regulation.[8] In 1970, for example, Nixon proposed to

---

5. "Social ideas," of course, was the polite way of referring to court-ordered racial integration. Quoted in *New York Times*, Oct. 4, 1968, p. 50.

6. *New York Times*, Nov. 3, 1968, p. 79.

7. Ambrose, *Nixon*, p. 202.

8. Numerous commentators have noted that Nixon's economic policies could have become the nucleus of a progressive modern Republicanism. See, for example, E. J. Dionne, Jr., *Why Americans Hate Politics* (New York: Simon & Schuster, 1991), pp. 193–200; Kevin

reform the welfare system through a guaranteed annual income, and in 1971 he imposed wage and price controls throughout the United States. On social issues Nixon moved to the right. His policy on civil rights was, in the words of Thomas and Mary Edsall, to develop "a strategy of staying within the letter of the law, while making abundantly clear wherever possible his reluctance to aggressively enforce it."[9] Nixon's response to the social and cultural revolution that swept America during the 1960s, however, was far less subtle. To the men of the Nixon White House, the rebellion on the campuses and in the streets was the result of rule by a rich, effete, liberal establishment, and they countered with unremitting hostility and contempt. Pragmatic economic policies coupled with social conservatism united the Republican party with the silent majority. In the hands of Richard Nixon, Republican control of the White House became a fiercely middle-class affair.

An important step in binding the South to the new Republican majority was to make good on promises regarding the Supreme Court. Lyndon Johnson had accepted Earl Warren's resignation subject to the confirmation of his successor; after the Senate's failure to confirm Fortas, Warren agreed to continue as chief justice until Richard Nixon could name a replacement. During the spring of 1969, as the Nixon administration considered candidates to replace Warren, rumors spread throughout Washington that Justice Fortas had engaged in financial dealings with Louis E. Wolfson, a wealthy financier convicted of violating federal securities law. In early May, *Life* magazine ran its famous story outlining the Fortas-Wolfson connection, and within a few weeks Fortas resigned from the Court.[10] Less than

---

Phillips, *The Politics of Rich and Poor: Wealth and the American Electorate in the Reagan Aftermath* (New York: Random House, 1990), pp. 39–42. Of course, the economic populism in the essentially pragmatic approach taken by the administration in domestic affairs was undercut by the venality of both Nixon and the political thugs he brought to the White House. The Nixon years produced several important accomplishments—the opening to China, for instance—but the student of American politics faces the inescapable conclusion that Nixon was a crook.

9. Thomas Edsall and Mary Edsall, *Chain Reaction* (New York: Norton, 1991), p. 81.

10. The story of the Fortas resignation is detailed in Murphy, *Fortas*, chap. 24.

six months into his presidency, Richard Nixon was blessed with the opportunity to fill two vacancies on the Court.

To replace Earl Warren, Nixon named Warren Burger, a law-and-order judge who had served on the Court of Appeals for the District of Columbia Circuit for thirteen years. In his judicial opinions and his off-the-bench writings and speeches, Burger had become a frequent, well-known critic of many Warren Court criminal process decisions, and his tough, at times strident views regarding the criminal process brought him to the attention of Nixon. Conservatives and southern Democrats in the Senate welcomed Burger with open arms. Robert Byrd, Democrat of West Virginia, for example, quoted with approval a 1967 Burger speech in which the soon-to-be chief justice questioned the sense of a criminal justice system that had as its primary goal the protection of citizens from police abuse rather than the protection of citizens from the criminal element.[11] Burger was easily confirmed, with only three senators registering negative votes.

To replace Fortas, Nixon sought a southern conservative; he nominated Clement F. Haynsworth, a court of appeals judge from South Carolina. "With this one," he was reported to have gloated, "we'd stick it to the liberal Ivy League clique who thought the Court was their own private playground."[12] Unmoved by the claims of civil rights organizations that Haynsworth was racially biased, the Senate appeared disposed to confirm, until hearings before the Senate Judiciary Committee revealed that Haynsworth had, at best, ignored or, at worst, actively avoided conflict-of-interest standards while ruling on several cases involving companies in which he held a financial interest. With memories of Fortas in the minds of senators on both sides of the aisle, Haynsworth was rejected by a vote of 55 to 45. Asserting that the Senate's action was simply another example of anti-South prejudice, Nixon vowed to continue his campaign to transform the Court. Although a setback to the administration, the rejection of Haynsworth probably enhanced the Republican resurgence in

11. See Leonard Levy, *Against the Law: The Nixon Court and Criminal Justice* (New York: Harper & Row, 1974), pp. 20–21, for a short description of the Burger hearings.
12. Quoted in Ambrose, *Nixon*, p. 296.

the South; nineteen Democratic senators, all from states below the Mason-Dixon line, cast votes in support of the nominee.

The nomination of G. Harrold Carswell following the defeat of Haynsworth showed—at least until Watergate, several years later—the Nixon administration at its worst. Carswell, described by Attorney General John Mitchell as "too good to be true," combined overt racism with marginal professional qualifications.[13] During his tenure as U.S. attorney in Florida, for example, Carswell helped in the assignment of a municipal golf course to a private club. The transfer of the city-owned facility, accomplished through a ninety-nine-year lease with rent of one dollar a year, was designed to avoid Supreme Court decisions outlawing segregation in publicly owned facilities. Later, when students at Columbia University Law School carefully reviewed Carswell's judicial career, they discovered an extraordinary reversal rate during his tenure as a trial judge. Distinguished legal scholars hammered away at the slender qualifications offered by the nominee.[14] On April 9, 1970, the Senate defeated the Carswell nomination by a six-vote margin. Again Nixon charged the Senate with "regional discrimination," maintaining that because of the Senate's intransigence he would be unable to name a southern conservative to the Court, and once again his administration gained stature and support in the South despite the defeat of the nominee.[15] Nixon's

13. After his failed nomination, Carswell ran in the Florida senatorial primary. He was photographed during that campaign with the sign "Heah Come de Judge" around his neck. Henry Abraham, *Justices and the Presidents*, 3d ed. (New York: Oxford Univ. Press, 1992), p. 18.

14. Provoking one of the most famous examples of senatorial idiocy on record, Roman Hruska, Republican of Nebraska, responded to the "mediocrity" claim of Carswell's critics by stating to a radio interviewer, "Even if he were mediocre, there are a lot of mediocre judges and people and lawyers. They are entitled to a little representation aren't they, and a little chance? We can't have all Brandeises and Frankfurters and Cardozos and stuff like that there." Quoted in Richard Harris, *Decision* (New York: Dutton, 1971), p. 110. This book remains one of the best case studies of the defeat of Carswell.

15. In subsequent elections one indirect result of the Haynsworth and Carswell votes became apparent. Democratic Senators Albert Gore of Tennessee and Joseph Tydings of Maryland were defeated by Republican opponents, and liberal Democratic Senator Ralph Yarborough lost to a more conservative Democrat in the Texas party primary. Their votes against Carswell were seen as important factors in their defeats.

nomination of Harry Blackmun, a moderate conservative from Minnesota, was approved by a vote of 94 to 0.

The defeats of Haynsworth and Carswell (as well as that of Fortas) signaled a dramatic change in the politics of judicial confirmation and were pivotal events in the evolution of the modern Republican party. Richard Nixon's "southern strategy" was a calculated effort to hasten the passage of southern whites to the Republican party. Attacks on the Supreme Court, both rhetorical and through the appointment process, were important ingredients in that strategy. Notwithstanding Nixon's outrage, the Haynsworth and Carswell defeats did little damage to the party's long-range electoral strategy; indeed, the twin setbacks confirmed the administration's commitment to make the white South a part of the Republican party. The Nixon administration's spin was to blame the defeats on a liberal elite's zealous defense of the judiciary as the instrument for imposing unwelcome social policies on the nation. The Supreme Court as the bastion of liberal elitism and the symbol of the retreat from fundamental American values, a metaphor artfully employed during the 1968 campaign, became Republican orthodoxy during the Nixon years and a powerful theme in the resurgence of the party.

Throughout Nixon's term in office, the judiciary remained a convenient scapegoat whenever the administration faced controversial policy choices. When, for example, intractable southern school districts continued to avoid the obligation to integrate, the Nixon White House chose lengthy court action rather than a speedy cutoff of federal funds (administered through the executive branch) as the appropriate federal response. Although leaders of the NAACP castigated Nixon for pursuing a policy of delay, the decision kept the administration within the confines of the law while refocusing southern attention on the courts and away from the executive branch. When Leon Panetta, then head of the Civil Rights Office in HEW, sought to answer the NAACP charges, John Ehrlichman of the White House staff told him to "cool it" and not challenge the NAACP interpretation of events. Panetta's conclusion was that the White House was not at all upset by the angry public reaction of the civil rights establishment.[16] The message to the white South was unmistakable: under the Republicans the executive branch would remain passive—and even encourage delay—in desegregating the South.

This strategic use of the federal courts to deflect the wrath of southern white voters proved quite successful. Among southern voters, Republican party registration increased along with expanded court-mandated integration. Southern politicians often went to great lengths to exonerate the executive branch and place responsibility on the Supreme Court for the changes in their constituents' lifestyles. After the executive branch joined the state of Mississippi in a futile attempt to delay the judicial implementation of a desegregation plan, Strom Thurmond announced, "The Nixon administration stood with the South in this case, but the Court has chosen to override the state of Mississippi and the Department of Justice."[17] With the judiciary the institution responsible for the integration of the South, the Nixon administration could escape the political consequences of a white backlash. Southern white support could be secured for the GOP, without significantly altering the inevitability of integration, by having the president denounce busing and affirmative action and by making promises and determined efforts to transform the Court through the appointment power. The strategy was extremely successful, and, whatever his motives, Nixon produced a minor political miracle; in 1972 southern whites' identification with the Republican party peaked, even though the South was far more integrated at the conclusion of Nixon's first term than at its beginning. By Nixon's second term making the Court a scapegoat had proven to be a surefire Republican strategy.

    16. A. James Reichley, *Conservatives in an Age of Change* (Washington, D.C.: Brookings Institution, 1981), p. 184.
    17. Quoted in James Simon, *In His Own Image: The Supreme Court in Richard Nixon's America* (New York: David McKay, 1974), p. 128.

CAPITALISTS AND FUNDAMENTALISTS

From Nixon to Reagan

In politics choosing one's enemies wisely often proves even more important than choosing one's allies carefully. In placing the responsibility for the ills of America on the Supreme Court, Nixon had found a villain without a voice of its own and with limited institutional capacity to defend itself and counter negative public opinion.[18] During a time of domestic upheaval and change, Nixon's unambiguous theme was that permissive judges had created a permissive society, and the message found a receptive audience. The Warren Court, at least in the view of its critics, was in the forefront of the dramatic changes sweeping America. Richard Nixon's message to middle America was that a change in the membership of the Supreme Court was a necessary first step in reestablishing in the nation a respect for the sacred institutions and traditions of American life and that as president he could be counted on to wage the long battle to transform the Court.

Watergate cut short the Nixon romance with middle America, exposing the paranoia and the amorality at the core of the man and destroying his presidency. Nevertheless, although Watergate did pave the way for the election of Jimmy Carter in 1976, it did not permanently derail the Republican national majority. When Ronald Reagan regained the presidency for the GOP in 1980, however, the party had a distinctly new "look."[19] The Republican coalition as envisioned by Nixon was anchored in middle America with a pro-

18. Historically the federal judiciary has relied on presidential support to counter political attacks. More recently the judiciary's linkages with powerful political groups— for example, the New Progressives—have increased its ability to withstand political retribution. In the late 1960s the New Progressives lacked the organization and political clout they enjoy today, and the Court's defenders were centered mainly in the civil rights community, a constituency that Nixon had long written off. See, generally, Mark Silverstein and Benjamin Ginsberg, "The Supreme Court and the New Politics of Judicial Power," *Political Science Quarterly* 102 (1987): 371–88.

19. This distinction is forcefully developed by Phillips, *Politics of Rich and Poor*, in chap. 2.

foundly middle-class social and economic outlook. Nixon's economic policy promoted state control and often drastically constricted the freedom of the markets; Kevin Phillips recalled that during the five years of the Nixon presidency there was little faith in the redemptive powers of unbridled capitalism.[20] It remained for Reagan to "unleash capitalism" and redirect national economic policy in favor of a capitalist elite. The 1980s became America's second Gilded Age; the rich got richer and the Reagan team dismantled the regulatory apparatus of the New Deal era, championing economic policies that advanced the concentration of wealth and ensured the victory of capital over labor. Upper-income taxpayers prospered, while lower-income Americans struggled to stay afloat and blue-collar jobs disappeared. The middle-class economic populism of Nixon gave way to the "country club" economic elitism of Reagan.

In short order, Reagan's ascendancy undercut any hope of a broad-based Republican economic populism. Moreover, "Reaganomics" posed at least a theoretical threat to a Republican revival by rewarding one part of the coalition (the entrepreneurial economic elites) at the expense of another (Nixon's forgotten American). A mark of Reagan's political genius was his ability to close this potential fissure by combining an abiding faith in the power and fairness of the financial markets with an embrace of the social values of a new movement within the Republican ranks. And an important part of Reagan's, like Nixon's, political wizardry lay in his capacity deftly to employ promises of an enduring campaign to recast the membership of the Supreme Court as the means of holding this most unlikely of coalitions together.

The New Right

Since the days of the New Deal, mainstream conservatives in the United States had stressed the twin themes of free enterprise on the domestic front and a strident anticommunism in international affairs. By the 1960s this brand of conservative politics was increasingly out

20. Ibid., pp. 35–36.

of touch with the needs and concerns of large numbers of American voters. In what amounted to a populist revolt against the blue-blood Republican establishment, a movement gathered force in the 1970s seeking to redirect conservative attention to "issues that people care about."[21] The New Right did not completely dismiss traditional Republican concerns, but the emphasis on the issues that people cared about—such as busing, abortion, pornography—and the skillful use of modern political technology connected these "new" conservatives with the blue-collar and ethnic American voter in ways that traditional conservatives could only imagine.

The New Right also sought to establish contact with a growing, but previously apolitical, evangelical movement.[22] Leaders of the New Right believed that a focus on the issues people cared about could be the glue that bound together the secular New Right, Protestant evangelicals, and conservative Catholics. A defense of Christian values and institutions fit easily into the agenda of the secular New Right, although it was ultimately a strident and uncompromising opposition to abortion rights that brought together the secular and religious movements. The organizational skills of the operatives of the New Right combined with the widespread appeal of television ministries to produce a potent political force, dedicated to mobilizing essentially blue-collar conservatives in a nationwide campaign to save the unborn, battle the moral relativism of modernity, and ensure the continued Republican hegemony in national politics.

In his drive to secure the Republican nomination in 1980, Reagan made an extended effort to court the New Right and link the evangelical movement to the Republican party. During the 1980 campaign the majority of fundamentalist leaders were outspoken champions of the

21. The words are those of Paul Weyrich, one of the foremost strategists of the New Right. Quoted in A. James Reichley, *Religion in American Public Life* (Washington, D.C.: Brookings Institution, 1985), p. 319. For an interesting essay comparing the New Right to the New Progressives, see Barbara Ehrenreich, "The New Right Attack on Social Welfare," in Fred Block et al., *The Mean Season: The Attack on the Welfare State* (New York: Pantheon, 1987).

22. The politicization of America's evangelicals is described in Kenneth Ward, *Religion and Politics in the United States* (New York: St. Martin's Press, 1987), chap. 7.

Reagan candidacy, and polls showed that on election day born-again Christians supported Reagan against the deeply religious Carter by a two-to-one margin. Evangelical churches became, in effect, the political "clubs" that impelled a Republican resurgence in the rural South. In the 1984 election white born-again Christians favored Reagan over Walter Mondale by a four-to-one margin.[23] Both the secular and the religious components of the New Right played significant roles in Republican victories during the 1980s, and the success of Ronald Reagan was due, in no small measure, to the fact that he stepped forward as the secular voice of a growing rebellion against the iniquities of modern life, a rebellion that found vivid expression in the religious revivalism of the last twenty years.[24] Focusing on the issues people cared about— abortion, prayer in school, pornography, traditional family values— paid huge electoral dividends and permitted Reagan to forge a strong bond with middle America. That it was Ronald Reagan—divorcé, irregular churchgoer, and longtime film actor in Hollywood—who became the herald of a return to traditional family values lends credence to the hackneyed observation that politics makes for strange bed-fellows.[25]

Conservative positions on issues like abortion and prayer in

23. It is important to remember that in the 1980 election Reagan's opponent was Jimmy Carter, a dedicated evangelical, who spoke publicly and sincerely of the importance of God in his public and private life. In the 1988 presidential election, George Bush, hardly one's image of a born-again fundamentalist, actually increased evangelical support for the Republican ticket.

24. The political impact of this religious revival has been the subject of several perceptive essays. See, for example, Walter Dean Burnham, "The 1980 Earthquake: Re-alignment, Reaction, or What?" in Thomas Ferguson and Joel Rogers, eds., *The Hidden Election: Politics and Economics in the 1980 Presidential Campaign* (New York: Random House, 1981); Alan Wolfe, "Cultural Sources of the Reagan Revolution: The Antimodern Legacy," in B. B. Kymlicka and Jean V. Matthews, eds., *The Reagan Revolution* (Chicago: Dorsey Press, 1988), pp. 65–81.

25. This was not the only contradiction inherent in the Reagan revolution. Reagan gave political expression to evangelical religious values while, at the same time, proclaim-ing a ferociously secular activity like venture capitalism to be the highest form of human endeavor. E. J. Dionne neatly captured another side of the contradiction: "Young invest-ment bankers who looked kindly on cocaine and fundamentalist factory workers who saw a world full of sin and corruption could vote for Ronald Reagan with equal enthusiasm. And they did." Dionne, *Why Americans Hate Politics*, p. 242.

school combined with the effective manipulation of patriotic symbols attracted to the GOP many lower-income voters severely bruised by Reagan's tax and income policy. Political scientists Benjamin Ginsberg and Martin Shefter have described a successful Republican strategy of transforming "workers to patriots" and "Southerners to evangelicals."[26] Republican anti-abortion rhetoric, for example, played equally well in rural, conservative Protestant churches and urban Roman Catholic districts; it permitted the party to "unite two forces—Catholics and Protestant evangelicals—that have been bitter opponents through much of American history."[27] Republican strategists unabashedly manipulated patriotic and military symbols to erode the traditional Democratic ties of blue-collar workers and southern whites; during the 1988 presidential campaign the American flag effectively supplanted the elephant as the symbol of the Republican party.

Like the Democratic coalition it succeeded, the Republican electoral coalition of the 1980s involved an attraction of opposites; it was anchored, on the one end, by lower- and middle-income northern ethnics and white southerners attracted by the conservative social policies advocated by Republican candidates and, on the other, by an economic elite generously rewarded by Republican tax and economic policy. In the Republican party evangelical voters play a role that mirrors that of black voters in the Democratic party, in effect forcing Republican candidates to the right and demanding explicit positions on controversial social issues.[28] On the other hand, high income is more closely associated with liberal than with conservative social

26. See Ginsberg and Shefter, *Politics by Other Means* (New York: Basic, 1990), chap. 4.

27. Benjamin Ginsberg, *The Captive Public: How Mass Opinion Promotes State Power* (New York: Basic, 1986), pp. 112–13.

28. In 1988 white evangelicals made up approximately 9 percent of the electorate, and slightly over 81 percent cast their vote for the Republican ticket. Blacks constituted 10 percent of the 1988 electorate and voted just over 85 percent Democratic. See Martin B. Wattenberg, "From a Partisan to a Candidate-Centered Electorate," in King, *New American Political System*, (2d version), pp. 139–74. The 1992 Republican platform and National Convention clearly indicate the power of the New Right in the national Republican party.

views, and, as a result, only a small percentage of the Republican economic elite share the social agenda of the secular and religious New Right.[29] Both Reagan and Bush faced a similar quandary: to push effectively the social policy program of the New Right risked alienating the economic well-to-do; to fail to produce legislative gains on a conservative social agenda invited potential discord on the right.[30]

Reagan: The Court as Alibi

The Nixon success in 1968 set the stage for a scenario in which the Supreme Court played the heavy for countless Republican office seekers. Placing responsibility for the ills of modern America on the federal judiciary deflected voter anger from the governing regime and became a proven Republican campaign theme. During the Reagan-Bush years the Court played an equally important but slightly altered role. Although the Reagan coalition could agree on the virtue of freeing capitalism from the vice of government regulation, the social agenda championed by the New Right contained the seeds of political disaster. Once again, however, the Supreme Court indirectly allowed Republicans to escape their own internal contradictions. In the most sublime of ironies, precisely the same Court decisions so easily reviled on the campaign trail were the decisions that would protect Republican presidents and legislators from the potentially disastrous electoral consequences of their enacting the social policy agenda of the New Right. Whatever the intensity of the chief executive's opposition to abortion, as long as *Roe* v. *Wade* remained good law, abortion rights were beyond presidential control. Reagan might promise to do all he could to return prayer to the classroom, but until *Engel* v. *Vitale* was overruled, the support remained rhetorical.[31] Indeed, almost all the social agenda championed by the New Right was governed by Su-

29. Ibid., p. 165.
30. The potency of a revolt from the right even to an incumbent Republican president is well illustrated by the discomfort Pat Buchanan caused George Bush during the early days of the 1992 primary season.
31. *Engel* v. *Vitale,* 370 U.S. 412 (1962).

preme Court precedent and thus removed from executive and legislative control.

The continuing force of many of the most controversial decisions of the Warren and Burger Courts permitted Reagan to retain the unquestioned loyalty of the right wing of his party through little more than a combination of pious rhetoric and promises to alter the makeup of the federal courts. Until a new conservative majority was installed on the Court, Republicans could hardly be held accountable for their failure to enact the new social agenda. Throughout the Reagan years the attention of the New Right was focused on the staffing of the federal judiciary; this produced significant political benefits for the administration. On the one hand, it marginalized the influence of the radical Right on domestic policy matters; without major changes in the federal judiciary and, in particular, the Supreme Court, sweeping social change was impossible. Until the judiciary was transformed, administration support for a pro-family, Christian moral and social agenda would be mainly symbolic. On the other hand, economic elites could easily support a Reagan presidency, secure in the knowledge that Supreme Court rulings on a host of privacy and First Amendment issues precluded enactment of the New Right's agenda. Winking at the language of the devout was a tiny price to pay for a reduction in marginal tax rates.

Success in American electoral politics has never demanded a high degree of internal logic, and throughout the 1980s Republicans continued to campaign to transform the federal courts even if the alliance that underwrote Republican victories could be maintained only so long as an active judiciary imposed a constitutional bar to the social radicalism of the New Right. During the Reagan years this preoccupation with judicial decisions and staffing kept the coalition together with little political cost. Although several leaders of the religious Right claimed that the administration failed to invest sufficient political capital in the battles to secure desired social legislation, evangelicals overwhelmingly supported Reagan's reelection in 1984. Jerry Falwell, of the Moral Majority, for example, closed the 1984 Republican convention with a benediction that heralded the party's candidates as "God's instruments in rebuilding America," and the campaign platform called for an end to abortion, defeat of the Equal Rights Amendment, and support of prayer in public schools.[32] Throughout the campaign and his final term in office, Reagan continued to speak the language of the pious, asserting that the Bible contained "all the answers to all the problems that face us today," but the energy of his administration was directed to the overwhelmingly secular matters of tax cuts, deregulation, and a military buildup to challenge the Soviets.[33]

Judicial Politics in the Reagan Era

The administration did not, however, completely abandon the legislative agenda of the New Right, particularly when the proposed action was of little concern to the remainder of the Republican coalition. For many years fundamentalists had clashed with the IRS over the tax-exempt status of church schools that discriminated against racial minorities. In 1982 Treasury Department officials announced that the IRS policy of refusing tax-exempt status for these religious schools would be revoked. Because the issue was then before the Supreme Court (the Carter administration had successfully defended the policy in litigation with Bob Jones University and the Goldsboro Christian School, and the schools had appealed to the Supreme Court), the Reagan administration moved to withdraw from the case, asked the Supreme Court to dismiss, and announced that both schools would be granted the requested tax exemption. The religious Right hailed the action, but civil rights groups fought back and secured a federal court injunction preventing the IRS from granting the exemptions.

The Reagan Justice Department responded by withdrawing its request for the Court to dismiss the Bob Jones and Goldsboro cases but announced that the government would appear on behalf of the two schools and not defend the IRS policy. The Supreme Court appointed William Coleman, a prominent private attorney, to argue

32. Wald, *Religion and Politics*, p. 194.
33. Quoted in Reichley, *Religion in American Public Life*, p. 325.

the IRS position, and the next year, by an 8-to-1 margin, it upheld the IRS regulations refusing tax exemptions to religious schools that practiced racial discrimination.[34] Although moderate Republicans may well have been embarrassed by the administration's heavy-handed efforts, the political cost was small, and, in the view of the New Right, Ronald Reagan had again fought the good fight against encroaching secular humanism and its champion—the U.S. Supreme Court.

To appease the New Right further and divert attention to the judiciary, the Reagan administration often demanded that government attorneys appearing before the Supreme Court urge upon the justices only the most conservative of legal positions. For example, during the 1984 term the Court confronted the issue of whether an Alabama statute setting aside one minute at the start of each school day for meditation or voluntary prayer violated the establishment clause of the First Amendment.[35] Attorney General Edwin Meese and other close Reagan advisers were reported to have pressured the solicitor general to urge upon the Court the proposition that the Bill of Rights did not apply to the states.[36] Such an argument, despite some historical validity and modern appeal to opponents of active judicial review, ran afoul of over fifty years of Supreme Court precedent and would not be accepted by the Court. Rex Lee, Reagan's first solicitor general, was placed in the uncomfortable position of having to refuse the administration's request to make the most extreme, doctrinaire arguments before the Court. "If I had done what was urged on me [by White House staff and Justice Department officials],"

34. *Bob Jones University* v. *U.S.*, 461 U.S. 574 (1983). The deputy solicitor general who signed the government's brief in the case arguing on behalf of the two schools noted in a footnote that, although he was signing the brief, he personally believed that the contrary position was the correct one. The remainder of the government attorneys who worked on the government's brief refused to sign it. For the complete story see Lincoln Caplan, *The Tenth Justice: The Solicitor General and the Rule of Law* (New York: Vintage, 1987), chap. 5; Elder Witt, *A Different Justice: Reagan and the Supreme Court* (Washington, D.C.: CQ Press, 1986), pp. 107–8.

35. *Wallace* v. *Jaffre*, 472 U.S. 38 (1985).

36. See Witt, *Different Justice*, p. 133, which presents an interesting review of the Reagan administration's legal strategy and the response of the Supreme Court.

Lee said, "I would have lost those cases and the Justices wouldn't have taken me seriously in others. There has been this notion that my job is to press the Administration's policies at every turn and announce true conservative principles through the pages of my briefs. It is not. I'm the Solicitor General, not the Pamphleteer General."[37]

Despite the harm it did to the solicitor general's credibility with the justices of the Supreme Court, the policy of urging the Court to reverse years of constitutional precedent produced political dividends, permitting Reagan to solidify his position as the champion of the New Right's social agenda. Moreover, the Court's reluctance to acquiesce in these extreme arguments ultimately enhanced the political rewards by allowing Reagan to assume this position without jeopardizing the support of the remainder of the Republican coalition.[38]

Equally important in securing the support of the religious Right without seriously imperiling the Republican coalition was Reagan's effort to transform the federal judiciary. Although all modern presidents have paid lip service to the importance of appointments to the federal bench, before the Reagan presidency executive scrutiny of potential nominees to lower federal courts was haphazard at best and limited by respect for senatorial patronage.[39] Under Reagan, however, the President's Committee on Federal Judicial Selection, consisting of key members of the White House staff and the Justice Depart-

37. Quoted in Caplan, *Tenth Justice*, p. 107. The solicitor general is appointed by the president and represents the government in cases before the Supreme Court. Because the United States is the most frequent party before the Court, the solicitor general occupies a unique position, representing the United States and yet serving almost as a "tenth justice," because the justices rely on the solicitor general's expertise and good faith.

38. The strategy may also have produced some anger on the part of at least three Reagan/Bush appointees to the Court. In *Planned Parenthood* v. *Casey*, 112 S. Ct. 2791 (1992), Justice O'Connor began her opinion, joined by Justices Souter and Kennedy, with the observation "The United States, as it has done in five other cases in the last decade, again asks us to overrule *Roe.*" The tone of Justice O'Connor's opinion suggests a good deal of frustration with Republican administrations for continually pushing the divisive abortion issue on the Court.

39. The classic study of the appointment process of lower-court federal judges is Harold Chase, *Federal Judges: The Appointing Process* (Minneapolis: Univ. of Minnesota Press, 1972).

ment, was formed to screen judicial appointments and allow the administration to apply a consistent ideological measure.[40] The selection committee conducted extensive interviews with prospective nominees to the federal bench, and the agenda of the New Right often formed the basis of the questioning. For example, Judith Whittaker, the associate general counsel to Hallmark Cards and highly rated by the American Bar Association, was rejected because she had supported the Equal Rights Amendment, and Andrew Frey, an assistant solicitor general, was turned down when his donations to Planned Parenthood and the National Coalition to Ban Handguns were discovered.[41] Although liberals and moderates complained that Reagan had introduced an "ideological litmus test" to the selection of judges, the New Right warmly endorsed the undertaking. The undeniable fact was that the Reagan administration had established the most comprehensive and effective process for recruiting and screening federal judges in the history of the American presidency.[42] And the minuscule political costs among mainstream Republicans were again more than offset by the political gains among the supporters of the New Right.

The campaign to change the ideological makeup of the Supreme Court was, of course, more visible. In naming the first woman to the Supreme Court, Reagan neutralized opposition from the Left but encountered some surprising opposition from the New Right. Sandra Day O'Connor was a moderate-to-conservative Arizona Republican, having served as a state legislator and appellate court judge. Warmly endorsed by many women's groups, O'Connor encountered New

40. For a review of the Reagan administration's procedures on judicial selection and their impact, see Sheldon Goldman, "Reaganizing the Judiciary: The First Term Appointments," *Judicature* 68 (1985): 313; Goldman, "Reagan's Second Term Appointments: The Battle at Midway," *Judicature* 70 (1987): 324.

41. See David M. O'Brien, "The Reagan Judges: His Most Enduring Legacy?" in Charles O. Jones, ed., *The Reagan Legacy: Promise and Performance* (Chatham, N.J.: Chatham House, 1988), p. 69.

42. See Stephan J. Markman, "Judicial Selection: The Reagan Years," in *Judicial Selection: Merit, Ideology and Politics* (Washington, D.C.: National Legal Center for the Public Interest, 1990), pp. 33–48, for a sympathetic description of the Reagan process of judicial selection.

Right opposition when it was discovered that as a state legislator she had favored a bill that would have repealed Arizona's remaining abortion laws and supported the Equal Rights Amendment. Her failure to take an unequivocal stand against abortion rights caused New Right conservatives in the Senate, led by Jesse Helms of North Carolina, to express grave misgivings about O'Connor, but in the end the Senate confirmed Reagan's first appointment to the Court with little debate.[43]

The elevation of William Rehnquist from associate to chief justice pleased most Republicans senators and southern Democrats but produced thirty-three negative votes on the floor of the Senate. Although Antonin Scalia sailed through with little opposition (in part because opposition from liberal groups concentrated on the effort to block Rehnquist), the battle lines were clearly and distinctly drawn over the nomination of Robert Bork to replace the moderate Lewis Powell. Bork possessed unquestioned professional and intellectual qualifications, as well as a judicial philosophy that squared neatly with conservative social views, and his appointment to the Court would have been the crowning achievement in the New Right's efforts to transform the Court.[44] So great was the New Right's rage over the

43. The hearings before the Senate Judiciary Committee were another matter and provided some melodrama. Senator Jeremiah Denton, Republican of Alabama, a favorite of the evangelical Right, was frustrated in his attempts to prod O'Connor to engage in a discussion of her views on abortion and complained, "I do not feel I have made any progress personally in determining where you stand on the issue of abortion." His Republican colleague Senator East of North Carolina, another voice of the religious Right, agreed and suggested that O'Connor's failure to answer their questions forthrightly undercut the Senate's role in the confirmation process. See Witt, *Different Justice*, pp. 40–41. Of course, in politics, as in life, what goes around comes around. A few years later, during the Souter and Thomas confirmation hearings, Democratic members of the Judiciary Committee expressed the same frustrations and misgivings, while conservative Republicans argued that attempts to question prospective nominees regarding their positions on abortion "politicized" the entire nomination process.

44. Those who maintained that the New Right may have lost the battle but ultimately won the war because Anthony Kennedy, the jurist confirmed in place of Bork, was equally conservative missed the significance of the Bork nomination and defeat. Bork's background, intellectual development, and personality suggested to many students of the Court that, once appointed, he would assume a leadership role on the Court, exercising great influence on the development of constitutional law for several decades. Justice

defeat of his nomination that the anger even spilled over to taint Ronald Reagan for what many considered his lackluster and detached efforts on behalf of Bork.[45]

REPUBLICAN ARMAGEDDON

End Game

In the 1988 presidential campaign George Bush promised a continuation of the Reagan policies, albeit in a more tempered and gentle manner. Ronald Reagan came to office with what was perceived as a powerful mandate for change and responded with bold initiatives that set the tone and tenor of his entire presidency. The Bush campaign of 1988, however, was lacking new ideas (but steeped in the symbols of patriotism, race, and crime), and Bush entered the White House with neither a personal agenda nor a real electoral mandate for altering existing policies. A cautious politician by nature, Bush was uncomfortable with ideological rhetoric, and his initial years in office were marked by an obvious attempt to avoid (at least in the realm of domestic affairs) major confrontations with the Democratic Congress. The most difficult problems facing the nation (escalating deficits, the cost and availability of health care, urban decay, and so on) were left untouched as the president pursued a risk-averse policy designed to lower the expectations of the electorate. In the aftermath of the Persian Gulf War, his popularity reached historic proportions. The epitaph for his presidency, however, might well be that in the last years of his term in office George Bush accomplished nothing with this popular mandate.

Kennedy is a competent jurist and *may* become a leader on the Court; Judge Bork, however, appeared *destined* to play such a role. Kennedy's refusal to vote to overrule *Roe* in *Planned Parenthood* v. *Casey*, 112 S. Ct. 2791 (1992) further vindicates the extraordinary effort of the New Progressives to defeat the Bork nomination.

45. See, for example, Patrick McGuigan and Dawn Weyrich, *Ninth Justice* (Washington, D.C.: Free Congress, 1990), pp. 220–21.

His long-term electoral strategy was similar to that of Reagan: keep in place Reagan tax and spending policies while courting the New Right through symbolic support of family values. The tangible rewards to the right wing of the party would be judicial appointments. The Reagan promise of transforming the federal courts through the appointment power would continue to be honored. The policy of appointing conservatives to the bench "was the greatest priority of conservatives who followed George Bush's election," noted Clint Bolick, a prominent New Right conservative who heads a group monitoring judicial appointments.[46] The two most important innovations during the Reagan era—the President's Committee on Federal Judicial Selection and the systematic screening of all potential nominees to the federal bench—were maintained by the Bush administration.[47] The profile of the typical Bush nominee to the federal bench was similar to that of the typical Reagan nominee. And the political impact of the appointments was to continue to fuse the Republican party's linkage with the New Right. "It's a very tasty morsel he gives to the rightwingers," said one judge (appointed during the Reagan-Bush era) of the Bush administration's efforts to appoint only the most conservative of jurists.[48]

During Bush's term in office the downside of this strategy became readily apparent. Throughout the 1980s Reagan skillfully used the staffing of the federal courts to quiet—and marginalize— the New Right. With the New Right preoccupied with the selection of judges, Reagan was free to go on in his secular quest to dismantle America's limited welfare state and erect Reaganomics as the centerpiece of a new entrepreneurial America. Until the judiciary was transformed, action on the politically divisive issues of school prayer, abortion, and racial integration could be postponed and energy and

46. Quoted in Neil A. Lewis, "Selection of Conservative Judges Guards Part of Bush Legacy," *New York Times*, July 1, 1992, p. A13.

47. See Sheldon Goldman, "The Bush Imprint on the Judiciary: Carrying on a Tradition," *Judicature* 74 (1991): 294, for a review of the first two years of the Bush administration's record on judicial appointments.

48. Quoted in Lewis, "Selection of Conservative Judges."

political capital concentrated on Reagan's economic program. By the time of the Bush presidency, decades of Republican appointments to the Court *had* altered the federal judiciary, enhancing both the expectations of New Right and the fears of socially moderate elements of the party. In his final years in office, Bush confronted what Reagan had long managed to avoid: a belief on the part of both critical wings of the Republican party that the constitutional constraints on the promotion of a new social agenda would soon be gone.

In the summer of 1989 the Supreme Court announced its decision in *Webster* v. *Reproductive Health Services.*[49] *Webster* had assumed unusual significance because it promised the first opportunity for Justices Scalia and Kennedy to make clear their positions on the abortion issue and perhaps to provide Justice O'Connor with the occasion to amplify her position on *Roe* as well. The drama was enhanced when the Court waited until the final day of the 1988 term of the Court to announce the decision. Although no one opinion commanded a majority and only four justices specifically recorded a willingness to overrule *Roe*, the tenor of the *Webster* decision appeared to indicate that the Court had turned a corner in the abortion debate, returning to the individual states substantial authority to restrict abortions.

The political fallout from *Webster* was considerable. Leaders of the evangelical and secular Right proclaimed that *Webster* was the long-awaited major victory and that the crusade to save the unborn and to redeem America was fast approaching a glorious conclusion. Pro-choice activists were galvanized into action, mobilizing their constituencies with the warning that no longer could the Supreme Court be relied upon to protect abortion rights.[50] The political direc-

---

49. 492 U.S. 490 (1989).

50. The reaction to *Webster* created a new abortion strategy. When the Supreme Court rendered the next long-awaited abortion decision, *Planned Parenthood of Southeastern Pennsylvania* v. *Casey*, 112 S. Ct. 2791 (1992), in which the Court again significantly cut back on *Roe* but pointedly refused to overrule that decision and return complete control of abortions to the states, both pro- and anti-abortion forces were quick to proclaim the decision a major *defeat* as a means for rallying their supporters. See Maralee Schwartz and Don Balz, "Preparing to Play Abortion Politics in an Election Year," *Washington Post*

tor of the National Abortion Rights Action League (NARAL) characterized the decision as "the smoking gun needed to mobilize our people."[51] Membership and contributions to pro-choice groups increased in the wake of *Webster*. Of utmost significance was the fact that the appeal to protect abortion rights resonated loudly within the ranks of moderate Republicans. In the 1989 New Jersey gubernatorial election, pro-choice Democrat James Florio soundly defeated Republican James Courtier, an opponent of abortion rights, and in Virginia, Democrat Douglas Wilder became the first elected African-American governor in the nation's history. In the cases of Florio and Wilder and in a host of other national, state, and local elections, exit polling indicated that the *Webster* decision and the intense political activity in its aftermath had energized a pro-choice majority that drew important support from segments of the Republican party.[52] In the words of Republican Senator Bob Packwood, Republicans in the 1989 elections "got the bejabbers beaten out of them because of abortion."[53]

Throughout the 1992 election season George Bush struggled to hold the Reagan coalition together. The religious Right, in the form of the Christian Coalition, under the leadership of Pat Robertson, supported Bush's reelection but warned that the failure to deliver on social policies and judicial appointments might result in the religious Right's sitting out the 1992 election. The *Webster* decision coupled with the Bush Supreme Court appointments of David Souter and Clarence Thomas (to replace Justices Brennan and Marshall, two of

---

National Weekly Edition, July 6–12, 1992, p. 8. Perhaps the real loser was George Bush. New Progressives announced that once again it was apparent that the overturning of *Roe* was only one vote away and that that was precisely what the upcoming presidential election was about. Important leaders of the New Right, characterizing the bloc of Justices O'Connor, Souter, and Kennedy that voted to retain the core constitutional principle of *Roe* as the "wimp bloc," called these appointments "an embarrassment to the presidents that appointed them." See Al Kamen, "Conservatives See a 'Wimp Bloc,' " ibid., pp. 7–8.

51. Quoted in Barbara Craig and David O'Brien, *Abortion and American Politics* (Chatham, N.J.: Chatham House, 1993), p. 296.

52. See ibid., chaps. 8 and 9, and Laurence Tribe, *Abortion* (New York: Norton, 1990), chap. 8, for a review of the impact of *Webster* on elections and on legislative politics.

53. Quoted in Craig and O'Brien, *Abortion and American Politics,* p. 299.

the strongest defenders of abortion rights on the Court) heightened the expectations of the religious and the secular Right. In an attempt to forestall even the hint of a rebellion from this part of the Republican coalition, Bush campaign advisers permitted the 1992 Republican National Convention to become a religious revival meeting, with the Bush-Quayle ticket anointed as God's champion in the battle against modernity and moral decay. From the more affluent and socially moderate members of the coalition, however, came the warning that the failure to temper the Republican party's conservative social agenda, particularly regarding abortion rights, would cost the party critical votes in key states such as California. In his struggle to hold the coalition together, Bush often appeared indecisive, without aim or direction. The New Right and the economic elites, always wary of each other, were equally uninspired by Bush, and a worsening economic situation and the candidacy of H. Ross Perot paved the way for Democratic victory.

The Loyal Opposition Once Again

A quarter of a century separates the fall of Abe Fortas from the tumult surrounding the Clarence Thomas appointment. During that period the changes in the politics of judicial confirmations served as dramatic illustrations of the vicissitudes of modern American politics. For all its significance, the Fortas defeat, in retrospect, was a relatively quiet affair. Television played a minor role, and the American populace remained uninvolved. But the battle over Fortas heralded a new type of confirmation politics. By the mid-1980s nominations to the federal bench often evoked the best and worst of modern American politics, as sophisticated media coverage and manipulation triggered mass participation in the selection of judges. In the midst of one of the most divisive Senate proceedings in modern memory, one participant described the process of Clarence Thomas's confirmation to the Supreme Court as "the worst kind of sleazy political operation."[54] Hyperbole

54. Senator John C. Danforth, Republican of Missouri, quoted in the *New York Times*, Oct. 9, 1991, p. A20.

aside, the description strikes home, if only because of the extraordinary participation of powerful groups of both political parties in a process often naively thought to be immune from politics as usual.

The election of Bill Clinton will not substantially alter the modern politics of judicial appointments. Although the positions will be reversed—the New Progressives will assume the role of recruiters of new judicial talent, while the New Right will provide the loyal opposition—the level of conflict and group participation is not likely to diminish. The pattern of modern American politics virtually assures contentious proceedings in the selection of federal judges. As New Progressives rejoiced with the election of Bill Clinton, the New Right formed the Judicial Selection Monitoring Project to monitor Clinton appointments and mobilize grassroots opposition.[55] Using high-tech media and communication advances (including a new cable television hookup designed to ensure an affiliate in every congressional district), the project hopes to coordinate New Right groups in a continuing campaign to contest the elevation of Democratic nominees to the federal courts. "I don't feel we have much of a choice," said Marianne Lombardi, the project's deputy director. "They're going to load up the courts with liberals and activists. We can't just stand by and let them do it."[56] The best-known supporter of the monitoring project is Robert Bork. In a fund-raising letter Bork sounded an ominous note to potential donors, asserting that "the judicial selection monitoring project is so vitally important to our nation's future" that, even before the first Clinton nominee is named, conservatives must organize and prepare to meet the coming challenge.[57]

55. See W. John Moore, "Judges on the Left! Hold That Line," *National Journal,* April 22, 1993, p. 1246.
56. Quoted in Ruth Shalit, "Borking Back" *New Republic,* May 17, 1993, p. 20.
57. See Neil A. Lewis, "Conservatives Set for Fight on Judicial Nominees," *New York Times,* Nov. 13, 1992, p. B16.

Chapter 5

THE SENATE: FROM MEN'S CLUB TO PUBLICITY MACHINE

The alteration of judicial power and the fragmentation of the governing coalitions over the last three decades continue to shape the process of selecting and confirming the justices of the Supreme Court. These developments must also be placed in the context of the changes that have taken place in the U.S. Senate over the same period. The "advice and consent" of the Senate is the final step in the confirmation process, and the transformation of the Senate from a hierarchical, inner-directed chamber to a more responsive and effective institution for the articulation of group interests has had a profound impact on the selection of judges.

In the aftermath of World War II, the New Deal coalition was firmly in place, judicial restraint was the guiding principle of judicial liberalism, and the Senate was an insulated and conservative institution in which a handful of senior members dominated the distribution of resources and widely accepted norms constrained behavior. These factors worked in concert to make the confirmation of a Supreme Court justice a low-key, predictable affair. By the 1960s, however, the Senate had begun a transformation as the accepted norms of Senate behavior lost their hold and the distribution of power and influence in the institution broadened. Individual senators became highly visible political actors, alive to the opportunity to champion the causes of citizens' groups with large, national constituencies. With the governing coalitions in disarray and the federal judiciary emerging as an important policy-making arena, the Senate provided a receptive forum for interests battling to control the shape and direction of the modern judiciary.

THE SENATE AT MIDCENTURY

The World's Greatest Deliberative Body

"[T]he Senate," wrote Alexis de Tocqueville, "contains within a small space a large proportion of the celebrated men of America. Scarcely an individual is to be seen in it who has not had an active and illustrious career. . . ."[1] His contempt for the more democratically elected House of Representatives, however, was unmistakable: "On entering the House of Representatives of Washington one is struck by the vulgar demeanor of the great assembly. Often there is not a distinguished man in the whole number. Its members are almost all obscure individuals, whose names bring no associations to mind. They are mostly village lawyers, men in trade or even persons belonging to the lower classes of society."[2] Tocqueville's aristocratic lineage and fear of a tyranny of the majority render his preference for the Senate hardly remarkable. Yet throughout a good deal of American history even those without his aristocratic predilections have found the Senate the more attractive chamber. There are many reasons for this preference, beginning with a senator's larger constituency and longer term in office. The disparity in the size of membership between the Senate and House, however, provides perhaps the most satisfying explanation. With over four times the membership of the Senate, the House utilizes strict rules limiting debate and equips its leadership with real authority over the prerogative of individual members. The greater the number in a legislative body, the more compelling is the need for rules of organization and procedure. Although such rules presumably advance institutional goals, they do, at least in the House, sharply curtail the power of a single representative to alter the course of legislation.

1. Tocqueville, *Democracy in America*, vol. 1 (New York: Knopf, 1956), p. 204.
2. Ibid. A reason that Tocqueville considered the Senate the more worthy chamber was that senators were appointed by state legislatures and thus freed from a direct connection with the petty concerns of constituency. An observer with greater sympathy for modern mass democracy might easily conclude that the Seventeenth Amendment enhanced Senate power by providing senators the legitimacy conferred by direct election.

The compactness of the Senate, however, demands less organization and permits greater independence for the individual legislator. Compared with those in the House, Senate leaders enjoy limited authority. A powerful Senate majority leader, for example, is nearly always a testimony to the leader's individual skills and personality, because the formal powers that attach to the post are minimal. Two recent majority leaders, Democrat Robert Byrd and Republican Robert Dole, both used the word "slave" in describing their experiences in the position.[3] Moreover, few, if any, legislative assemblies in the world encourage individual autonomy and free debate to the extent the U.S. Senate does. The Senate, in short, as an institution venerates the prerogative of the individual senator and, because of its permissive rules and flaccid organization, during the twentieth century emerged as the arena where the ambitious can make a difference and become figures of national repute and importance. It is therefore hardly surprising that promising members of the House usually harbor aspirations at one time or another of joining "the greatest deliberative body in the world."

The Folkways of the Senate

One might expect in an institution that proudly retains a tradition of unlimited debate, minimal formal leadership, and membership autonomy a good deal of conflict over matters as weighty and potentially divisive as appointments to the Supreme Court. For a substantial part of the twentieth century, however, conflict was the exception rather than the rule. Despite the long tradition of members' independence, throughout much of this period the Senate was a comparatively cohesive, self-contained, and efficient legislative body. The lack of

3. Dole's predecessor as majority leader, Howard Baker, Republican of Tennessee, was less melodramatic when he characterized the leadership position as essentially "janitorial" in nature. See Roger Davidson, "The Senate: If Everyone Leads Who Follows?" in Lawrence C. Dodd and Bruce I. Oppenheimer, eds., *Congress Reconsidered*, 4th ed. (Washington, D.C.: CQ Press, 1989), pp. 275–306. Affirming the theme of this chapter, Professor Davidson concludes that, even with limited formal powers, today's Senate leaders are less likely to assert control than the leaders of the post–World War II era were.

strict procedural regulations led to a highly developed pattern of unwritten rules and norms that governed behavior in the institution and stifled the independence of members. "There is great pressure for conformity in the Senate," reported one of its influential members during the early 1950s; "it's just like living in a small town."[4] And in the small town that was the Senate of the 1950s, the unwritten but well-understood rules of conduct virtually guaranteed that such potentially polarizing issues as the appointment of judges would not be permitted to disrupt the orderly flow of Senate business.

In his pioneering study of the Senate of the 1950s, Donald Matthews stressed the significance of what he termed the "folkways of the Senate" in structuring behavior within an institution whose organization and formal rules exalted the unfettered autonomy of each of its members.[5] Matthews reported, for example, that every new senator was expected to serve a period of apprenticeship. The apprenticeship norm required younger members to remain subservient to their more experienced colleagues, postponing for a substantial period full participation in the legislative process while learning the ways of the Senate. Admonished not to appear too aggressive, newcomers thus often avoided engaging in floor debates during their initial years in the Senate. Slots on important committees went to senior members; newcomers had little control over their own fate, invariably serving the bulk of their apprenticeship on the least-desirable committees. The new arrival was expected to seek the advice of older senators and, with some luck, might become the protégé of a powerful colleague, hastening the end of the apprenticeship period and the junior member's ascent of the rigid hierarchy of the Senate. "Like children, we should be seen and not heard," observed one senator of the norm of apprenticeship.[6]

One consequence of the apprenticeship system was to dimin-

---

4. Quoted in Matthews, *U.S. Senators and Their World* (Chapel Hill: Univ. of North Carolina Press, 1960), p. 92.

5. Ibid., chap. 5. Much of the material that follows regarding the folkways of the Senate of the 1950s is drawn from this work.

6. Ibid., p. 93.

ish significantly the number of senators likely to play important roles in controversial matters. This effect was enhanced by the general expectation that the primary concern of a senator was to be the work of the Senate. Although the need for favorable publicity was acknowledged to be part of public life and thus unavoidable, the folkways of the Senate dictated that the quest for public acclaim always be kept secondary to the work of the institution. To showboat and to court unduly the attention and accolades of the press was to risk the disdain of one's peers. In stark contrast to the ethos of today's Senate, the norms of this era gave rise to an institution where the respect and influence accorded a senator by colleagues tended to vary inversely with the degree of media attention and publicity attracted by him or her.

Thus the most influential and important senators, in the view of their fellows, were those who developed areas of expertise and dedicated substantial time and effort to specializing in one sphere of legislative activity. By midcentury the quantity of complex legislation confronting the Senate demanded a division of labor, and the committee system, buoyed by the norm of specialization, assured senators that, before reaching the Senate floor, proposed legislation had undergone the scrutiny of peers who had spent years becoming expert in the relevant policy areas. In this highly structured world a few senators might manage to acquire influence beyond their area of expertise (Richard Russell being the perfect example), but this unusual power invariably rested on a generally acknowledged base of specialization.[7] Although "playing to the galleries" by speaking out on a broad range of issues might gain a senator public attention, such behavior ran counter to well-established norms and was almost certain to earn the gadfly the contempt of colleagues.

Professor Matthews described an institution in which reciprocity was a way of life. Senators were expected to aid their colleagues whenever possible, and a bargain struck was a bargain kept. By

---

7. Barbara Sinclair, *The Transformation of the U.S. Senate* (Baltimore: Johns Hopkins Univ. Press, 1989), p. 18.

demanding a deference to the decisions of the relevant committees, reciprocity reinforced the norm of specialization and made unruly floor fights rare events. Furthermore, reciprocity became the lubricant that prevented the antiquated gears of the Senate from sticking. The rules and traditions of the Senate entrusted in the individual member enormous power to bring the work of the chamber to a complete halt.[8] The spirit of reciprocity proscribed the exercise of that power in all but the most extraordinary cases. Any senator who pursued personal goals through the use of these draconian powers would be breaking a widely accepted norm of behavior and inviting retaliation from other senators. When coupled with the convention of courtesy (for example, refraining from personal attacks, always complimenting colleagues, avoiding outward manifestations of partisanship) and institutional patriotism (always being protective of the Senate as an institution), these folkways formed a powerful check on the behavior of most of the members of the institution and provided the Senate with the coherence and structure necessary for the efficient operation of any lawmaking body.

The self-regulating effect of these norms was reinforced by the political makeup of the post—New Deal Senate. During the 1940s and 1950s membership in the Senate was divided almost equally between Democrats and Republicans; not until 1958 did the Democrats establish a lopsided majority. The equality of the parties produced a decidedly conservative Senate. Southern Democrats often teamed with Republicans to form a conservative majority that effectively controlled the operation of the institution. Southern states, with all white Democratic electorates, repeatedly reelected Democratic senators, and Senate norms and the rules of seniority guaranteed these

8. Matthews suggested several examples of this power. The filibuster remains, of course, an obvious one. Much of the Senate work on the floor is done under unanimous-consent agreements, which supplement or substitute for the standing rules and often are designed to limit debate and floor amendments. Unanimous-consent agreements can be adopted only if no senator objects; a single senator, simply by objecting to all unanimous-consent agreements, can bring proceedings in the Senate to a virtual halt. Furthermore, a single senator can sneak measures through by acting when few others are in attendance on the floor of the Senate. See Matthews, *U.S. Senators*, p. 100.

men positions of influence. Republicans of the era were always conservatives. Thus no matter which party formed a narrow majority, the conservative coalition dominated the Senate and a disproportionate share of power rested in the hands of conservative Senate elders. These men—Richard Russell and Everett Dirksen, among them—profited the most by the general acceptance of the Senate norms and, not surprisingly, manipulated the resources of the institution to ensure their vitality. In the Senate at midcentury a set of rules of behavior and control of the institution by a conservative oligarchy went hand in hand.

The norms of the Senate were also in basic harmony with the political world in which the typical senator lived and worked. Despite the general trend of the twentieth century toward the centralization of power in Washington, D.C., this process was (and continues to be) a gradual one, and for a good part of the century the jurisdiction of the national government was, by today's standards, limited. The narrow range of federal activity curbed the number and variety of private interests seeking to influence national lawmaking. Moreover, not long ago most states had a relatively homogeneous population, and the typical senator served a constituency with only a handful of major policy concerns. The broadcast media were in their infancy, and a senator had few opportunities to seize a highly visible issue and ride it to national prominence. Of necessity, and with few exceptions, senators responded to stimuli within the institution; the Senate of this era was, in the words of one prominent scholar, a "self-contained, self-regulating, inward-looking institution."[9]

In such a political setting the cost to the individual member of following Senate norms was not great.[10] Committee assignments, for example, could be more easily tailored to constituency needs, and therefore specialization often aided and rarely hampered reelection.

9. Richard F. Fenno, "The Senate through the Looking Glass: The Debate over Television," in John Hibbing and John Peters, eds., *The Changing World of the U.S. Senate* (Berkeley, Calif.: IGS Press, 1990), pp. 184–85.
10. See Sinclair, *Transformation of the U.S. Senate*, chap. 2, for an interesting discussion balancing the costs and advantages of adherence to the Senate norms.

The narrow scope of federal legislation and the limited activity of organized interests provided little impetus for the typical senator to defy the unwritten rules of the Senate and seek fame and glory outside its confines. On the other side of the ledger, abiding by the norms promised a senator a satisfying career in a predictable and stable setting. Even the most junior of senators might be beguiled by the prospect of rising through the hierarchy and someday assuming a leadership position, and this could be accomplished only by playing strictly according to the rules. Although the net effect of the Senate norms was virtually to guarantee that most senators toiled in relative obscurity, the benefits of maintaining the norms for most members far outweighed the cost of being a maverick.

The Cost of Being a Maverick: The Case of Hubert Humphrey

Nevertheless, the rules of conduct were not universally accepted; the Senate has always had its share of nonconformists. Professor Matthews identified several factors that limited the universality of the norms.[11] People who achieved political prominence in another setting before coming to the Senate, for example, inevitably had difficulty working within the constraints of the Senate folkways. Political ambition also weakened the force of the norms on some senators; those with dreams of the presidency typically sought greater national visibility than Senate norms allowed. Nonconformity was also more prevalent among senators who represented states with diverse, heterogeneous populations where fierce two-party competition made reelection a constant concern. Constituency pressure was particularly a problem for "liberal" or "progressive" senators. Elected to office by voters expecting dramatic legislative action, liberal senators confronted a conservative institution that demanded the postponement, if not the total surrender, of a personal legislative agenda. For obvious reasons, conservatives found the Senate a more hospitable environment.

11. Matthews, *U.S. Senators*, pp. 102–17.

The experiences of Senator Hubert Humphrey during this period illustrate the difficulty of challenging the clubby atmosphere of the old Senate. A well-known progressive, Humphrey became a player in midwestern politics when he successfully negotiated the alliance between the militant Farm-Labor party of Minnesota and the Democratic party. A lifelong advocate of activist government, Humphrey was one of labor's most forceful champions and a passionate supporter of civil rights policy. Elected mayor of Minneapolis in 1945, the dynamic Humphrey virtually dominated post–World War II politics in Minnesota. In 1948, while a candidate for a U.S. Senate seat, Humphrey addressed the Democratic National Convention in support of a minority resolution seeking to add a civil rights plank to the party platform. His speech—only eight minutes long—electrified the crowd, and, in a stunning upset, the resolution passed despite the opposition of southern delegates.[12] The convention speech catapulted Humphrey into the national limelight, with Democrats in the South castigating him as a dangerous demagogue and progressives welcoming the voice of a resurgent liberalism.

Humphrey's pre-Senate political experience was that of a dynamic, hands-on executive of a large city, and on the eve of his arrival in Washington he had already experienced the flush of national prominence. As the spokesman of the Democratic Left, he naturally expected to pursue his progressive agenda and his own political career in a national forum. Following his election to the Senate, for example, Humphrey accepted the chairmanship of the Americans for Democratic Action. The ADA had been founded a few years earlier

---

12. Indeed, Humphrey's address to the Democratic convention, in hindsight, might be considered one of the more important moments of America's twentieth-century political history. It decisively placed the national Democratic party in support of civil rights. Following the speech, delegates from four southern states bolted the convention and later nominated Senator Strom Thurmond as the Dixiecrat candidate for president. From the moment of Humphrey's speech through the 1960s, the links between the Democratic party and the white supremacist South became increasingly tenuous, because, in the words of his biographer, "Humphrey's speech and the vote that followed nailed civil rights to the masthead of the Democratic party and set the nation, as well as his party, on a new course." Carl Solberg, *Hubert Humphrey: A Biography* (New York: Norton, 1984), p. 19.

by liberal New Dealers who believed that the Democratic party was drifting to the right and becoming a party of reaction. The organization sought to influence national Democratic party politics, and Humphrey's willingness to head the organization on the eve of his arrival in the Senate made him the spokesman for an organization with a broad national agenda. Today a similar position gains the neophyte senator prestige and national visibility; in 1948 it guaranteed the wrath of Senate elders.

With an abundant faith in the virtues of activist government and a burgeoning national reputation, Humphrey felt little inclination to adapt to the ways of the Senate. He considered himself competent to speak on a range of problems and did not hesitate to express his views on the floor of the Senate. When Senate leaders treated him like a newcomer, Humphrey responded by charging that too many Senate elders were too beholden to powerful interests. He directly challenged the Senate seniority system and scorned the norm of apprenticeship; during his first year in the Senate, he offered fifty-seven bills, spoke out on some 450 different topics, and filled the *Congressional Record* with insertions.[13] The Senate hierarchy did not take kindly to such assertiveness by a newcomer. Not one measure he introduced was enacted, and despite his national reputation, his dynamic style, and his boundless energy, Humphrey soon became an isolated figure in the Senate.

By 1950 he was so frustrated that he attacked Harry Byrd of Virginia, one of the Senate whales. Byrd, a conservative Democrat, headed the Joint Committee on Non-Essential Expenditures, a committee created primarily to permit Byrd to voice his contempt for government spending through a steady stream of press releases. A local Minnesota group, working with the Byrd committee, had gathered statistics vastly inflating the potential cost of measures proposed by Senator Humphrey and released the numbers to the Minnesota press. When Humphrey spoke out against Republican efforts to slash federal spending, Republicans sought to use the statistics to embarrass

13. Ibid., pp. 143–45.

Humphrey and impeach his credibility on economic matters. Unwilling simply to refute the statistics, Humphrey counterattacked, describing the Byrd committee as a waste of taxpayers' money and a perfect example of the nonessential expenditure of federal funds. Although in private few would have disagreed with this assessment, Humphrey's statement was taken as a personal attack on a powerful, senior member of the Senate. To make matters worse, not only had a freshman senator challenged a pet project of a Senate whale, but the attack had taken place while Byrd was out of town visiting a sick relative and unable to defend himself on the floor of the Senate.

A few days later Byrd responded to Humphrey. Following Byrd's remarks the senior members of both parties each, in turn, castigated the upstart newcomer. The humiliation of Hubert Humphrey on the floor of the Senate lasted for over four hours. When Humphrey finally was recognized and rose to speak, the Senate whales marched out of the chamber. He had become quite simply a Senate untouchable. Bobby Baker, a longtime aide to Lyndon Johnson, described the event rather starkly: "Humphrey made a big mistake when he first got to the Senate. He got up and said that Senator Harry Byrd of Virginia was a no-good sonofabitch, and they almost kicked him out of the Senate for that."[14]

Later one of Humphrey's aides reported that newly available information substantiated his charges against the Byrd committee, and he urged his boss to remain on the offensive. Humphrey declined; he had learned his lesson. "I found out where the power was in the Senate," Humphrey recounted in his autobiography, "and I found out what you could expect when you challenge that power frontally."[15] The transformation of Hubert Humphrey into a highly effective member of the Senate was aided immeasurably by Lyndon Johnson. Although LBJ had arrived in the Senate the same year as Humphrey, he quickly developed an instinctive feel for the institution and its mem-

14. Merle Miller, *Lyndon: An Oral Biography* (New York: Putnam, 1980), p. 154.
15. Hubert H. Humphrey, *The Education of a Public Man* (Garden City, N.Y.: Doubleday, 1976), pp. 130–31.

bers. His basic message was simple; the path to power in the U.S. Senate was to do things "their" way. Influence and prestige coupled with the ability to move legislation could be attained only through an acceptance of the folkways of the Senate and not in defiance of them.[16] Johnson's willingness to help Humphrey was itself a lesson in the ways of the Senate; Johnson had designs on becoming the Senate Democratic leader, and by cultivating Humphrey he could establish a link to the small band of Democratic Senate liberals. As for Humphrey, with Johnson's tutelage, he became a more effective senator. "I've stopped kicking the wall," he said, in regard to his transition.[17]

The Old Senate and the Old Politics of Judicial Confirmations

The agonizing education of Hubert Humphrey as a U.S. senator not only sheds light on the Senate of the 1950s but also provides a powerful explanation for the high success rate enjoyed by presidents in obtaining Senate confirmation of Supreme Court nominees for two-thirds of the twentieth century.[18] During Humphrey's first years in the Senate, the surest path to influence and power in the institution was to gain the respect of colleagues. Much to Humphrey's discomfort, gaining it demanded submission to the folkways of the Senate;

16. In the words of longtime political commentators Rowland Evans and Robert Novak, Johnson "gave Humphrey a short course on the Senate and how it really functioned. He explained the importance of knowing the strengths and weaknesses of every Senator, of concentrating on committee work and of mastering a speciality." Evans and Novak, "Lyndon B. Johnson: The Ascent to Leadership," in Norman Ornstein, ed., *Congress in Change: Evolution and Reform* (New York: Praeger, 1975), p. 128.

17. Quoted in Solberg, *Hubert Humphrey*, p. 164. Until his death, in 1978, Humphrey pursued an extraordinary career in public service, with the Senate as a principal base of operations. In fact, Humphrey proved to be one of the first of a new breed of senator, combining a mastery of the inner workings of the Senate with a broad focus on national issues.

18. From 1900 to 1968, apart from the rejection of Judge Parker in 1930, the Senate confirmed every nominee. By way of contrast, during the nineteenth century the Senate rejected one out of three nominees to the Court. The Senate of that era was a more partisan institution. With senators appointed by state legislatures—the Seventeenth Amendment was ratified in 1913—powerful state party leaders often found their way to the Senate and used it to funnel patronage back to the state party organization. The typical senator of the nineteenth century had a secure local power base and little tolerance for institutional norms that constrained individual behavior.

nonconformists might achieve a certain prominence (Humphrey's first, futile years in the Senate, for example, did not preclude him from continuing as a nationally recognized champion of liberal causes), but isolation in the institution and limited legislative effectiveness would inevitably be the costs. Political life always demands an appreciation of the cost and benefits of action; one of Humphrey's most important lessons was that influence in the Senate was a finite resource to be cultivated and conserved for the battles that might really matter.

In the Senate at midcentury, however, the confirmation of federal judges was often a battle that did not matter and thus presented senators with a relatively simple decision. With few exceptions, appointments to the Supreme Court were of little electoral import to senators. After the constitutional revolution of 1937, the attention of the New Deal coalition shifted from the judiciary to the administrative state, and, until the Warren Court revolution of the 1960s, the nature of judicial power did not make judicial appointments critical events for potent political forces. Rarely would an appointment even to the Supreme Court attract the attention of a senator's constituents; it is probably safe to say that from 1900 through 1967 not one senator's career was enhanced or cut short by constituent response to a confirmation vote.

In the self-contained world of the Senate, such freedom from electoral retribution yielded more rather than less conformity. For the typical senator of this era, pursuing an independent course on the consideration of a Supreme Court nominee presented few tangible benefits; conforming to the expectations of colleagues in the institution, however, would almost certainly further other personal and political goals. If the leaders of the Senate were satisfied with a judicial nominee, there was simply nothing for the average member to gain from challenging that conclusion.

Considered from this perspective, LBJ's strategy in the Fortas nomination made perfect sense.[19] He consulted with the appropriate

19. One student of the confirmation process has concluded that Johnson mismanaged the Fortas nomination, stressing his decision to consult with only a few Senate elders and the resulting failure to accurately assess the mood of the Senate. See John Massaro, *Supremely Political: The Role of Ideology and Presidential Management in Unsuccessful*

Senate elders, and he used the extensive resources of the executive branch to cultivate these votes without public scrutiny or participation. The conduct of affairs within the Senate had always depended on informal, personal agreements made among the whales, and their ability to manipulate the resources of the Senate, coupled with the moderating effect of the Senate norms, always produced a stable and predictable pattern of behavior. It was unthinkable, for example, that a group of renegade young Republicans would defy Everett Dirksen, particularly on a matter of so little significance to constituents. In terms of the traditional Senate norms, such behavior made no sense. In the Senate of Lyndon Johnson, where formal norms protected the status quo and where members were continually encouraged to seek the approval of their peers and discouraged from pursuing undue national exposure, the odds overwhelmingly favored a president in the confirmation process.

THE SENATE TODAY

A New Political World

"Being in the U.S. Senate," reports Arkansas Senator David Pryor, "is like getting stuck in an airport and having all your flights canceled."[20] Pryor's reproach is echoed by many of his colleagues, although their criticisms often lack his gentle, homespun touch. Whereas senators once spoke in reverential tones of "the world's greatest deliberative body," today's senator is more likely to describe chaos and anarchy and complain of the trivial nature of much of the work. The senator of an older generation often spoke warmly of his colleagues as "the

---

Supreme Court Nominations (Albany: SUNY Press, 1990), chap. 2. In retrospect this conclusion appears unassailable. One might also conclude, however, that Johnson, lacking the wisdom provided by hindsight, conducted the Fortas nomination with an understanding of the well-established folkways of the Senate. The "mismanagement"—if that is the appropriate term—was the failure of Johnson in 1968 to grasp the extent to which new forces were undercutting the old norms and reshaping the Senate.

20. Quoted in Hedrick Smith, *The Power Game* (New York: Ballantine, 1989), p. 26.

best men in political life."[21] Nowadays senators are more apt to agree with Warren Rudman's unsenatorial portrait of his colleagues: "One third of the members of the U.S. Senate know why they're here, know what they want to do, and how to do it. The second third know why they're here and what they want to do, but don't know how to do it. And that last third, I'm not sure why they're here."[22] The Senate norm of institutional patriotism, demanding that senators revere the institution and its personnel and champion both in the outside world, has obviously fallen upon hard times. In fact, few, if any, of the norms described by Professor Matthews in his study of the Senate of the 1950s compel the same allegiance today.[23] The erosion of these folkways has transformed the institution, producing a new Senate populated by a new type of senator. One consequence of this transformation has been to alter the politics of judicial confirmations dramatically.

The first challenge to the inner-directed world of the Senate came from a profound change in membership. The late 1950s were difficult years for Republicans. In 1957 President Eisenhower suffered a stroke, and, despite his recovery, his health continued to haunt Republican politics. In 1958 scandal surfaced in the White House when Chief of Staff Sherman Adams accepted gifts from a businessman, Bernard Goldfine, and intervened with the Federal Trade Commission to discuss a case involving Goldfine. Marines were sent to Lebanon, and voters grew uneasy over the threat of another foreign war. A recession took a heavy toll on the prosperity of many Ameri-

21. See Matthews, *U.S. Senators*, p. 102, for an example of how senators of the 1950s spoke of the institution and their colleagues.

22. Quoted in Smith, *Power Game*, p. 673. Rudman, expressing a frustration with the political process that carried well beyond the confines of the U.S. Senate, announced in 1992 that he would not seek reelection despite a highly favorable reputation among New Hampshire voters.

23. The best single discussion of the changes in the modern Senate appears in Sinclair, *Transformation of the U.S. Senate*. None of the discussion that follows is intended to suggest that senators never express allegiance to the old norms or that those norms are currently without effect. Rather, the norms today are simply more honored in the breach than in the observance. See Fred R. Harris, *Deadlock or Decision: The U.S. Senate and the Rise of National Politics* (New York: Oxford Univ. Press, 1993).

cans. The congressional elections of 1958 reflected the Republican decline. In the House, Democrats won a 283-to-153 majority; in the Senate, Democrats gained 13 seats, bringing their total to 64. Many of these new Democrats were liberal northerners; Edmund Muskie of Maine, Philip Hart of Michigan, Eugene McCarthy of Minnesota, and William Proxmire of Wisconsin were among the new Democrats in the Senate who would rise to prominence in the 1960s. Frustrated with the ways of the old Senate, the new liberal contingent set out to reform the institution. Although their initial efforts failed—in January of 1959, for example, southerners led by Richard Russell defeated attempts to liberalize cloture—the locus of power in the Senate began to shift.

The change in membership was symptomatic of other developments in the body politic that eventually converted the Senate from a tightly organized, self-regulating institution to a more fluid body, populated by members with an acute appreciation of the political world beyond the Senate chamber. The New Deal gave momentum to the centralizing forces in the American system, and by the 1960s the expanded agenda of the national government produced a prodigious increase in the number of interests groups seeking access to national arenas of power. The growth was particularly evident in the number of citizen groups—those organizations open to all, regardless of occupation and status and concerned primarily with broad "quality of life" or public-interest issues.[24]

Although any interest group welcomes friendly voices in the Senate, the typical citizen group makes the Senate the focal point of its most intense lobbying efforts. "[I]ssues with national implications,"

24. Obvious examples of such groups include Common Cause, the Sierra Club, and the National Organization of Women. The links between many of these groups and the New Progressives are quite evident, and their prominence produced a reaction and countermobilization on the part of groups associated with the New Right. In addition, business interests responded to the success of citizen groups by increasing their presence in Washington, D.C. On the explosion of group interests, see, for example, Kay Lehman Schlozman and John T. Tierney, *Organized Interests and American Democracy* (New York: Harper & Row, 1986); Jeffrey Berry, *The Interest Group Society* (Boston: Little, Brown, 1984).

writes Professor Ross Baker, "as opposed to more detailed and technical legislation [are] best pursued in the Senate. . . . If you can infuse
one of the senators with passion for your cause and convince him or
her that great policy consequences can be read in it, the senator can
be an estimable catalyst and attract national attention."[25] The prolifer-
ation of citizen and public-interest groups undercut the inward-looking stability of the old Senate not merely by increasing the demands
on senators but also by expanding greatly the opportunities for a
senator to achieve national prominence outside the institutional confines of the Senate.

As Barbara Sinclair has noted, the Senate began its transformation in the 1960s when the constellation of political forces rendered
the old norms obsolete and provided senators with many new ave-
nues to political success.[26] Chief among the new forces altering the
world of the Senate was the rapid growth of the electronic media. It
would be difficult to overstate the effect of the mass media on
American politics; documenting this effect has become a veritable
cottage industry for countless scholars and political commentators.
Most of their efforts center on assessing the electoral repercussions
of the media explosion. Whether the outcome of elections may be
altered by media coverage or the manipulation of images by the
candidates remains a subject of legitimate inquiry.[27] The conventional
wisdom is that media coverage has a significant impact on who wins
and who loses in American politics, and this perception creates its
own reality.

As a consequence, the media do not merely report on modern
politics but have become an integral part of the political process. Their
impact is most easily observed in the modern presidency. A powerful
explanation for the "imperial" presidency in the post—World War II

25. Baker, *House and Senate* (New York: Norton, 1989), p. 166.
26. Sinclair, *Transformation of the U.S. Senate*, chaps. 4 and 5.
27. See Doris Graber, *Mass Media and American Politics* (Washington, D.C.: CQ
Press, 1989), for a review of the relationship between the media and politics. Thomas
Patterson, *The Mass Media Election* (New York: Praeger, 1980), assesses the effect of the
media on the 1976 presidential election.

era is that the presidency, centered on one individual, is far easier to package for the visual image than is an institution as large and diverse as the Congress. Television has also supplanted the political party as the primary link between the people and the politicians. Who needs a strong party organization to ring doorbells when an appearance on television will bypass the front door and put you in thousands of living rooms? The reality of the power of the media produced a new breed of legislator, skilled in the use of modern technology to enhance political power. A special telegenic charm and wit and the ability to speak in ten-, twenty-, or thirty-second sound bites are the qualities most cherished by a new generation of political leaders.

In the Senate increased media attention diluted the force of the traditional norms and encouraged a new style of behavior.[28] At the core of the older Senate was the belief that prestige and power came to those who earned the respect of their colleagues in the institution. The established norms required senators who wished to achieve influence to conform to the expectations of other senators. The media explosion dramatically altered the Senate ideal, replacing the behind-the-scenes specialist with the highly visible, and quotable, generalist. The escalating costs of reelection campaigns reinforced this evolution, encouraging senators to attract out-of-state contributions by expanding, rather than narrowing, their scope of activities. Because national prominence is now an alternative path to power and influence in the

28. See, for example, Gregg Easterbrook, "What's Wrong with Congress?" *Atlantic*, Dec. 1984, p. 26; Michael Robinson, "Three Faces of Congressional Media," in Thomas Mann and Norman Ornstein, eds., *The New Congress* (Washington, D.C.: American Enterprise Institute, 1981), pp. 60–99. Stephen Hess, by contrast, concludes that the media focus on the small number of senators in leadership positions and therefore cannot be charged with producing the decentralization of power in the institution. Hess, *The Ultimate Insiders: U.S. Senators and the National Media* (Washington, D.C.: Brookings Institution, 1986). Even Hess's study confirms that senators (both junior and senior) with a flair for the media can become a presence on national television. A fascination with the *national* media, however, should not obscure the obvious growth of local news outlets and the obsession of officials in Washington with the need to have their words and faces beamed back to the folks at home. Although not as dramatic as an interview with Dan Rather, favorable local coverage is considered absolutely necessary for reelection. The technological advances that expand the breadth and sophistication of local media coverage intrude on the traditionally insular nature of the Senate and alter the behavior of its members.

Senate, enhancing the chances of reelection as well as a run for higher office, the modern, well-financed senator strives to achieve a public voice on a broad range of policy questions.

A classic example of such behavior took place in 1985 when the Senate Commerce Committee held hearings on the problem of "porn rock" and the advisability of compelling recording companies to provide warnings on the album covers of records containing violent or sexually explicit lyrics. Although the hearings featured appearances by Dee Snider (of the heavy metal band Twisted Sister) and rock icon Frank Zappa, the real star of the proceedings was first-term Senator Paula Hawkins, Republican of Florida. Neither a queen of rock nor a member of the Commerce Committee, Hawkins nevertheless requested the opportunity to testify, and she came equipped with her own television monitor to show rock videos (including Van Halen's "Hot for Teacher") as well as blowups of "explicit" album covers. Hawkins's multimedia performance caught the attention of the networks, and portions of her testimony appeared on two of the national nightly news programs. Not so long ago newcomers to the Senate would not even have dared to dream of such wide exposure.[29]

The Minnows Have Swallowed the Whales

Television has dramatically altered the folkways of the Senate. At midcentury the limited concerns of constituency and the jurisdiction of committee defined a senator's policy agenda. Today pervasive electronic media coverage makes highly visible activities like contesting the nomination of a Supreme Court nominee a normal—and often necessary—event in a senator's life. One casualty of the seemingly endless effort by senators to be heard on a wide range of issues is the primacy of the committee system. Although committees remain a vital arena of legislative activity, committee assignments can no

---

29. Smith, *Power Game,* pp. 119–21. In addition to the appearance on the national news, Hawkins, who was involved in a tough reelection campaign, made sure of local coverage by "feeding" the tapes of her performance to thirty local Florida stations through a satellite hookup provided by the Senate Republican Conference.

longer even pretend to exhaust the modern senator's policy interests. Because more senators wish to be heard on a substantial number of issues, debates on the floor of the Senate, rather than behind-the-scenes work in committee and subcommittee, increasingly dominate the lawmaking process. Amendments from the floor, for example, are now frequent and expected, and they often come from junior senators who are not even members of the committee that originally reported the legislation.[30]

The norms and Senate rules that relegated junior senators to a marginal Senate role have largely been abandoned. Today the Senate newcomer enters the chamber with a complete legislative agenda and fully expects to be involved directly in the legislative process. A minor skirmish during Pennsylvania Republican Arlen Specter's first term in office illustrates this development.[31] In his second year in office Specter sponsored a nonbinding resolution requesting the president to convene a summit meeting with the Soviets in the hopes of limiting the arms buildup.[32] Senate elders on both the Foreign Relations Committee and the Armed Services Committee opposed the resolution. When Specter, despite his freshman status, refused to defer to the leadership, Republican John Tower, the powerful chair of the Armed Services Committee, enlisted senior members of the committee as well as the White House to pressure the upstart. Before the Senate vote Tower announced to the members that both the Armed Services Committee and the Foreign Relations Committee were opposed to the resolution. Specter refused to back off, demanding that the secretary of the Senate check the precedents for similar informal

30. Sinclair, *Transformation of the U.S. Senate*, pp. 80–84, quantifies this development.

31. Richard Fenno, *Learning to Legislate: The Senate Education of Arlen Specter* (Washington, D.C.: CQ Press, 1991).

32. "This kind of nonbinding resolution is a favorite of individual senators who want to convert a personal opinion of some sort into an opinion of a Senate majority, hoping to focus interest, attract publicity and, if possible, influence behavior. The resolution is merely an expression of opinion; it requires no action by any committee; it cuts across the normal flow of legislative business; its passage forces no implementation and no official need act on it. Because it is an opinion, however, and because it often disrupts normal procedures, it may stir controversy." Ibid., p. 80.

statements of committee position and challenging Tower on the Senate floor about whether it was actually he or the committee that opposed the resolution (Tower admitted the former). Privately, Specter lobbied his younger colleagues for their votes, in effect championing the new individualistic ethic of the younger senators against the traditional powers of the Senate whales. The effort paid substantial dividends, though the resolution, which did pass, had no substantive effect on policy. In the eyes of his colleagues and the press, Specter had effectively "beaten" the powerful John Tower and, in so doing, enhanced his image both inside and outside the Senate.[33]

In the old Senate the brazen defiance of elders by a newcomer was not tolerated. Today, however, the norms that often stifled independence and cast senators like Hubert Humphrey in the role of mavericks are of marginal influence. The qualities displayed by Senator Specter during the skirmish over the summit resolution are hardly unique; independence, assertiveness, and a willingness to defy the Senate leadership are characteristics found today in many senators. In the contemporary Senate, leaders rarely express surprise when a junior member takes center stage or when colleagues are deeply involved in issues that fall outside the jurisdiction of their committees. The Senate's traditional, hierarchical structure at mid-century is no more.

Even the formal rules governing the structure of the Senate reflect these developments and now disperse power throughout the institution. Reforms instituted during the last twenty-five years permit senators to serve on only one of the more prestigious committees

33. Ibid., pp. 79–86. Another newcomer able to influence major policy decisions was Senator Phil Gramm, Republican of Texas. Elected to the House in 1978 as a conservative Democrat, Gramm switched parties, won election to the Senate in 1984, and in his first year in the Senate cosponsored the famous Gramm-Rudman bill, which established a schedule of automatic budget cuts designed to produce a balanced budget. Not only did Gramm in his first year in office sponsor perhaps the most hotly debated piece of legislation of recent years, but his rather arrogant demeanor and abrasive personality hardly made him the most popular of colleagues in the Senate. Gramm became a major player despite his junior status and his personality. See Alan Ehrenhalt, *The United States of Ambition: Politicians, Power, and the Pursuit of Office* (New York: Times Books, 1992), pp. 227–28.

(Appropriations, Armed Services, Finance, and Foreign Relations); as a result, 80 percent of the members now hold a seat on one of these committees. The limit on the number of committees a senator may chair and the increase in the number of subcommittees give more senators the opportunity for committee and subcommittee leadership. Both parties have modified the previously inflexible rule of seniority in the selection of committee chairmen, and within the committee the autocratic power of the chairmen has been tempered. That most meetings must now be open to the public, coupled with the ever-expanding television coverage of C-Span, makes it easier for even the most junior senator to become a public personality while pursuing policy goals.

In addition, the huge growth in personal and committee staff permits individual senators to spread themselves continually thinner, delegating responsibilities and relying on the expertise of staff members across a wide range of policy areas. Highly trained lawyers and policy analysts on Senate staffs render the specialization norm passé. There is little to be gained in spending years in Senate solitude on a quest for knowledge and experience when expertise is easily hired and senators are left free to pursue more visible, career-enhancing activities. The erosion of the specialization norm further weakens the committee system; the advent of the generalist not only challenges the primacy and exclusive authority of the appropriate standing committee but also directs attention away from the committee to the more egalitarian forum of the Senate floor. In sum, the ability to influence legislation is distributed evenly throughout the Senate, no longer correlated with longevity and formal position in the institution.

Other norms significant merely a generation or two ago also play a diminished role. Because the new generalist seeks to exert influence on a wide range of legislation, the Senate floor has become a critical playing field in the policy game. With activity on the floor thrust into the spotlight, the norm of courtesy and civility has suffered. Invective and thinly disguised personal insult often mark debate in the modern Senate.[34] Institutional patriotism has given way to a rash of critiques of both the institution and fellow senators; self-promotion and the quest for personal advancement are not easily compatible with strong institutional loyalty. What most disturbs Senate elders, however, is the obvious fact that the vast power of the individual member to obstruct Senate proceedings has now become a viable and often used tactic for enhancing personal influence and prestige.

The filibuster, for example, once employed almost exclusively by Senate conservatives in their battle against civil rights legislation, is currently employed or its use threatened by senators of diverse ideologies to further personal goals.[35] Conservative Republican Jesse Helms of North Carolina and liberal Democrat Howard Metzenbaum are two well-known senators who have little in common other than a willingness to use the Senate rules to advance their own agenda.[36] Although neither Helms nor Metzenbaum would win a popularity contest among their peers, they apparently suffer few, if any, consequences for their defiance of the Senate norms. Indeed, although the Senate continues to be an institution where members fashion legislative deals and honor commitments, it is also one where, increasingly, an individual member's power to say no defines the workings of the legislative process.

34. Consider this exchange during the floor debate over the nomination of Clarence Thomas to the Supreme Court. Senator Kennedy, responding to claims that Anita Hill perjured herself while testifying against Thomas, asserted, "There is no proof that she has perjured herself and shame on anyone who suggests she has." Senator Orrin Hatch responded, "Anybody who believes that, I know a bridge up in Massachusetts that I'll be happy to sell them." Hatch was obviously attempting to embarrass Kennedy by reference to the car accident at Chappaquiddick in 1969.

35. Sinclair, *Transformation of the U.S. Senate*, pp. 94–95.

36. Metzenbaum is famous for his end-of-session "watchdog" filibusters. As the Senate hurries to adjournment, senators often push through bills favoring particular constituents. Metzenbaum refuses to cooperate in this classic example of "reciprocity," prompting Senator Ted Stevens to label him a "pain in the ass." Metzenbaum also does not hesitate to engage in "filibuster by amendment," a process by which he ultimately kills bills by offering a slew of germane and nongermane amendments. See Smith, *Power Game*, pp. 62–63.

A NEW SENATE AND THE NEW POLITICS OF
JUDICIAL CONFIRMATION

A New Ball Game on a New Playing Field

The Senate of the 1950s was stable, predictable, and, for the most part, sheltered from the winds of change that might batter a more democratic institution. Not surprisingly, judicial confirmations of the same era were often uneventful and unaffected by partisan politics. The tradition of seniority, the explicit division of labor, and the disproportionate distribution of resources combined with the folkways of the institution to guarantee the White House that any nomination would be contested on a playing field screened from public view, the number of important players would be small, the rules of the game rigid and strictly enforced, and the outcome reasonably predictable.

With members' attention directed inward to the institution, the Senate promoted efficiency by curtailing the number of influential actors on any policy matter and, not coincidentally, closing off the world's foremost deliberative body from many of the nation's most pressing concerns. (Witness, for example, Richard Russell's famed ability to keep civil rights legislation from coming to a floor vote.) The influential few were inevitably institutional conservatives, dedicated to maintaining the ways and norms of the Senate and ready to manipulate the allocation of resources to reward the conformist and punish the heretic. In such a setting Senate elders were often able to deliver votes, and the cultivation of a few important senators, along with an abiding respect for the ways of the institution, formed the core of a successful strategy to manage any Senate vote.

The contemporary Senate presents a distinctly different picture.[37] The norms of an earlier era no longer curb the behavior of

37. Norms in an institution such as the Senate always develop and influence behavior, and the modern senator thus is not totally free from their constraints, a point emphasized by Fred Harris in *Deadlock or Decision*, especially chap. 4. Although the

individual senators; the result is a far less stable, more outward-regarding institution and a more complicated process of securing the Senate's consent to a judicial nomination. Increased media coverage and the constant search for campaign funds invite independent action and encourage senators to become visible players in matters of national interest. Televised committee hearings diminish the ability of the leadership to control the proceedings, making the outcome far less predictable to friend and foe alike.

Beginning in the late 1960s the dynamics of party politics and the changing nature of judicial power combined to make appointments to the Supreme Court very significant to powerful political forces. At the same time, the Senate has become a more open and visible forum for the expression of diverse interests than it was even a generation ago. Activists in both political parties now find important and vocal allies in the Senate; the New Progressives and the New Right have proven equally adept at cultivating senators to champion their respective causes. For the typical senator identification with national issues that transcend state or regional boundaries is the cornerstone around which a triumphant senatorial career is now built, assuring the senator prestige in the institution, visibility among the folks back home, and, perhaps, a national following. For example, Senator Robert Griffin of Michigan was a little-known first-term Republican senator when he defied Everett Dirksen and led the insurgent Republicans against the Fortas nomination. Following his successful challenge to Fortas, Griffin was elected to a Senate leadership position and quickly emerged as a national spokesperson for an independent federal judiciary. During the Haynsworth nomination fight, Griffin was a key player, assiduously courted by both sides. After deciding to cast his vote against Haynsworth, he was character-

---

scholarly and journalistic inclination to underscore the conformity of the Senate of the 1950s and the individualism of the Senate of the 1980s might result in some exaggeration, the fact remains that "change" is a repeated theme in the literature discussing the modern Senate.

ized by several prominent observers, including the *New York Times*, as among the most influential opponents of the nominee.[38]

It makes equally good sense for groups engaged in the policy process to court influence with senators. Interests broadly identified with the New Progressives or the New Right, for instance, prefer a senator to a member of the House of Representatives as the "symbol" or "spokesperson" of the group not simply because of the Senate's constitutional role in the confirmation process but because senators tend to attract greater media attention. The Senate has become the most accessible institution for those seeking to influence the national political agenda, with a membership acutely sensitive to the concerns of outside groups that champion causes with a national appeal. Increasingly this means that the proponents and opponents of any nomination will have willing advocates in the Senate.

A New Political Calculus

The fact that politically powerful groups are willing to invest substantial time and resources in the battle to control the judiciary, coupled with the erosion of the old Senate norms and the appearance of a new Senate style, has altered the political calculus for every senator confronting a vote on a nominee to the federal bench. Throughout much of the twentieth century, a senator could simply conform to the expectations of peers and accept the president's choice. The nomination of even a Supreme Court justice was of no electoral consequence, and thus the safest vote, in terms of the expectations of Senate leadership and presidential patronage, was usually a yes vote. In the contemporary Senate, however, to be counted for or against a particular nominee is often a decision of immense electoral significance, and each senator is keenly conscious of the potential consequences of such highly visible activities.

In 1969, when Abe Fortas resigned from the Court following the *Life* magazine article detailing his connection with financier Louis

38. John Frank, *Clement Haynsworth, the Senate, and the Supreme Court* (Charlottesville: Univ. of Virginia Press, 1991), p. 89.

Wolfson, Richard Nixon delivered on his "southern strategy" by nominating Clement Haynsworth, a native of South Carolina and a judge on the Court of Appeals for the Fourth Circuit.[39] Opposed from the outset by labor and civil rights groups, Haynsworth nevertheless presented solid legal credentials and appeared a safe bet for confirmation until the Judiciary Committee hearings revealed the conflict-of-interest improprieties that doomed the nominee. The opposition seized on the alleged improprieties to capture media coverage and focus public attention on the proceedings. Significantly the opposition was led by Birch Bayh, Democrat of Indiana, a little-known second-term senator who, as a direct result of his efforts to defeat Haynsworth, established a national reputation as a leader in the civil rights and labor movements. Once the public interest was engaged, senators on both sides of the aisle were forced to reassess their original reflexive support for the nominee and measure their position against the expectations of constituents and important interest groups.

The White House responded with heavy-handed attempts to mobilize public support for Haynsworth and to increase pressure on recalcitrant senators. Southern state Republican leaders were asked to generate letter-writing campaigns stressing that Haynsworth was being attacked because of his ties to the South, and the White House lobbied large campaign contributors of key senators.[40] When the administration's letter-writing campaign appeared to be faltering, Nixon directed his staff to get in touch with Gerald Ford (then the House minority leader) to try to begin impeachment proceedings against William Douglas, the most liberal member of the Court. The obvious message to liberals was that Justice Douglas would be the price to be paid if Haynsworth were defeated.[41] The Nixon White

39. See chapter 1, n. 22.

40. John Anthony Maltese, "The Selling of Clement Haynesworth: Politics and the Confirmation of Supreme Court Justices," *Judicature* 72 (1989): 338.

41. Stephen E. Ambrose, *Nixon: The Triumph of a Politician, 1962–1972* (New York: Simon & Schuster, 1989), p. 315. The investigation of Douglas revolved around his connections with a foundation from which he received $12,000 a year as well as around

House in this way raised the perceived stakes for each senator by injecting a still larger dose of politics into the process while publicly castigating opponents of the nomination for employing similar tactics. In the end, the efforts of groups opposed to Haynsworth to shape public opinion were successful, and Richard Nixon, still fresh from his presidential victory a year earlier, was unable to control the vote of seventeen Republicans. The nomination was defeated by a vote of 55 to 45.

In the years since the Fortas and Haynsworth confirmation fights, the politics of judicial confirmations have grown ever more complex. Consider, for example, the political calculations of southern Democrats in the Senate during the Bork proceedings. At the outset many of these conservative Democrats appeared to welcome a Bork nomination to the Court. At a minimum, Bork was an unrelenting critic of the judicial activism that had been anathema to the white South since the days of the *Brown* decision. Furthermore, the religious Right overwhelmingly supported Bork, and evangelicals constitute a powerful electoral force in southern elections. Few observers of the political scene, therefore, were exactly thunderstruck when Richard Shelby, a newly elected Democratic senator from Alabama, enthusiastically supported Robert Bork, commenting that if Ted Kennedy was against the nomination "a lot of us southern Democrats will have to be in bed with Bork."[42]

Shelby's ardor for Judge Bork, however, quickly cooled. As a member of the House of Representatives, Shelby had developed a reputation as a conservative on racial issues, voting, for example, against an extension of the Voting Rights Act and against the proposed Martin Luther King holiday. Stepping up to run for the Senate in 1986, he needed substantial black support to defeat the reactionary Republican incumbent, Jeremiah Denton, in a closely contested elec-

---

his "radical" writings. The House Judiciary Committee actually investigated the matter, and it came to nothing. See William O. Douglas, *The Court Years: The Autobiography of William O. Douglas* (New York: Random House, 1980), chap. 15.

42. Ethan Bronner, *Battle for Justice* (New York: Norton, 1989), pp. 285–88.

tion. The approximately 90 percent of the black vote that Shelby received was, no doubt, attributable only to the notoriety of his opponent; the newly elected Senator Shelby could not expect similar black majorities in future campaigns against more moderate opposition unless he tempered his own voting record. Three months of intense lobbying and polling data indicating a good deal of black opposition to Bork apparently convinced Shelby that a vote for the conservative Bork might considerably shorten his own Senate career.

Other southern Democratic senators experienced a similar conversion. The resurgence of the Republican party in the South makes Democratic electoral success often dependent on the black vote. In the battle over Bork southern Democrats in the Senate were sensitive to the lobbying efforts of black organizations and aware that polls showed substantial African-American hostility to the nomination. The result was that southern Senate Democrats formed a solid bloc (save for Ernest Hollings of South Carolina) voting against confirmation. Republicans, on the other hand, saw the Bork vote as an opportunity to solidify support among southern whites. In the days preceding the Senate confirmation vote, the question arose whether Bork should withdraw his name and avoid a crushing defeat on the Senate floor. Several key Senate Republicans (including Republican leader Robert Dole) urged him to stand firm, forcing Democrats like Shelby to cast a vote against Bork. The Republican leadership thought that the cost of such a vote to southern Democrats among white voters would more than offset the possible gain among black constituents.[43] The lesson of the Bork battle was not lost on the strategists of the Bush presidency. Intent on placing a New Right conservative on the Court, the White House settled on Clarence Thomas as part of a strategy to gain the votes of southern Democratic senators by marshaling the support of black voters.[44]

43. See Mark Gitenstein, *Matters of Principle* (New York: Simon & Schuster, 1992), p. 301.
44. The strategy worked. As was noted, only one southern Democrat, Ernest Hollings, voted for Bork. In the case of Thomas, Hollings was joined by John Breaux and John Johnston of Louisiana, Sam Nunn of Georgia, Charles Robb of Virginia, and Shelby

The current reality is that the confirmation process now demands a calculation of political variables so complex that even the most experienced and electorally secure senators are often unable to predict the course and outcome of the proceedings. This was not always true. In 1916, following the confirmation of Justice Brandeis, the incumbent Woodrow Wilson faced Charles Evan Hughes (who had resigned from the Court to accept the Republican nomination) in a hard-fought presidential election battle. The confirmation battle played no visible role in the presidential campaign, and there is no evidence that senators on either side of the nomination battle faced significant voter recrimination. Seventy-five years later, however, the Clarence Thomas proceedings seriously damaged George Bush's reelection bid. More significant, perhaps, in terms of the Senate's understanding of the electoral impact of Supreme Court confirmations, was the primary defeat of a Democratic incumbent senator, Alan Dixon of Illinois, by a virtual political unknown, Carol Moseley Braun. Braun, the Cook County recorder of deeds, decided to enter the Democratic primary after Dixon voted to confirm Thomas, and voter discontent with the Dixon vote powered her campaign. In Pennsylvania, Arlen Specter, the leader of the Republican counterattack against Anita Hill, faced a potent reelection challenge by Lynn Yeakel, another political unknown inspired to run against a powerful incumbent by the Thomas hearings. Although Specter survived the challenge, the experiences of Specter and Dixon remain stark reminders to every senator of the potential electoral consequences of modern confirmation battles.

The confirmation of Clarence Thomas was, of course, not the

---

of Alabama. Given the 52-to-48 margin of victory, the votes of these senators were of obvious significance. Prior to Anita Hill's allegations of sexual harassment, Thomas's key backer in the Senate, John Danforth of Missouri, predicted that sixty or so senators would vote to confirm (which, of course, would still have been a narrow margin of victory). Without the complications of the Hill testimony, more southern Democrats would have supported Thomas. For example, Senator Robert Byrd of West Virginia, who gave an impassioned speech on the Senate floor opposing Thomas, inserted into the record the speech supporting Thomas he would have given had he not believed Hill's allegations.

whole explanation for the substantial gain in female representation in Congress.[45] Nonetheless, the unforgettable images of the Thomas hearings served to emphasize the institutionalized gender inequality and insensitivity that galvanized so many of the campaigns run by women candidates. Increasingly confirmation proceedings highlight themes that evoke powerful reactions from the public at large, and the changes that have taken place in the folkways and rules of the modern Senate make the members sensitive to shifts in the mood of the electorate. The history of confirmation battles from Fortas to Thomas shows the ability of powerful forces to make the confirmation of Supreme Court justices turn on the electorate's responses to highly charged issues of public and social policy, and the transformation of the modern Senate virtually guarantees that this strategy will continue.

45. In 1992, 11 women ran for the Senate and 106 for the House. Four new women senators were elected (for a total of 6), and the election produced 24 new women representatives (for a total of 47). See Marian Lief Palley, "Elections 1992 and the Thomas Appointment," *Political Science and Politics*, March 1993, pp. 28–31.

CONCLUSION: THE DEMOCRATIZATION OF THE CONFIRMATION PROCESS

In January of 1993 retired Justice Thurgood Marshall died of heart failure, at the age of eighty-four, and America paid final tribute to an extraordinary man of the twentieth century. He reached the very pinnacle of power in the United States and yet, unlike many in public life today, never forgot where he came from. Justice Marshall was also possibly the last of a succession of justices whose appointment to the Court followed a long and distinguished career in the public service. It would scarcely be a disservice to the memory of Justice Marshall to suggest that his greatest contributions came well before his appointment to the Court, during his years as the attorney for the NAACP leading the historic legal campaign to end apartheid in America. In the twilight of the twentieth century, we can look back and say with confidence that Marshall was America's greatest public lawyer. Had he never attained a seat on the Supreme Court, his place in history would still be secure.

The twentieth century has seen others like Marshall who accomplished much before ascending to the high court. Oliver Wendell Homes, Jr., wrote over one thousand opinions as a judge on the Supreme Judicial Court of Massachusetts, published the classic *The Common Law*, and emerged as America's foremost legal thinker before his appointment to the Court at age sixty-one. Although he served for thirty years as associate justice, the case could be made that

Holmes did his finest work prior to his years on the Supreme Court. His friend and colleague Louis Brandeis was considered by many America's foremost lawyer before his appointment to the Court in 1916, achieving almost mythical status as "the people's attorney" and the champion of progressive causes.

Charles Evans Hughes came to the Court in 1910, after serving as governor of New York. He resigned in 1916 to run for the presidency, losing that year's presidential election to Woodrow Wilson by a mere twenty-three electoral votes. He later served as U.S. secretary of state before his appointment as chief justice 1930. William Howard Taft, of course, was president of the United States before achieving in 1921 the position he coveted—the chief justiceship. Benjamin Cardozo was America's most respected state court judge before his appointment, and his successor, Felix Frankfurter, while still a professor at the Harvard Law School, was described in 1936 by *Fortune* magazine as "the single most influential individual in the United States." Earl Warren was both governor and attorney general of California and Thomas Dewey's running mate in the 1948 election before he was tapped to be chief justice by President Eisenhower. Harlan Fiske Stone, William O. Douglas, Robert Jackson, and Abe Fortas also could be counted among the twentieth century's best-known nominees to the Court.

These men, irrespective of personal politics or judicial philosophy, were among the best and brightest of their generations. They came to the Court with unquestioned personal stature and achievement and amid widespread public anticipation that they would have a profound impact on the development of American constitutional law. Their appointments were the outcomes of a predictable and stable process controlled, for the most part, by legal and political elites. Today, however, the system of judicial confirmations is a far more democratic process, shaped by extraordinary public participation and media coverage, and one might do well to ponder whether such a process is likely to produce appointmentees of similar talent and distinction. On occasion those of limited experience or parochial background may while serving on the Court grow into giants of

American law, just as the nominee of great standing may prove a disappointment. Nevertheless, the conclusion that must be drawn from the preceding pages is that the contemporary confirmation process is not configured to favor nominees to the Court with the stature of a Frankfurter or a Holmes or the legendary experience of a Brandeis or a Marshall.[1]

A half century ago the process was predictable and stable, controlled by insiders and cut off from public participation. Gaining the support of a few key actors all but guaranteed confirmation. In such a setting, deals could be cut and votes traded to secure the confirmation of an eminent nominee, no matter the long paper trail and abundance of political enemies associated with a career in public affairs. By the same token, similar deals could be cut to elevate political hacks and cronies. For every Brandeis and Frankfurter, the process also brought forth a McReynolds or a Whittaker.[2] From the turn of the century through 1968, the staffing of the Court depended on the good will, vision, and political acumen of a small handful of men, and the lack of public participation produced nominees that ran the gamut from the truly inspirational to the simply wretched.

In 1968 the defeat of Abe Fortas stunned many astute observers

1. Unless such a nominee possesses additional qualities that might neutralize the expected opposition. If a nominee of stature is, because of color or gender (or both), treated with greater deference than a distinguished white male, then perhaps the modern confirmation, for all its flaws, has achieved a kind of rough justice.

2. James McReynolds was appointed by Woodrow Wilson in 1914 and served for twenty-seven years. He was a reactionary, a misogynist, a racist, and an anti-Semite. He often would leave the conference room when Brandeis spoke, and he read a newspaper during the swearing-in ceremony for Cardozo while muttering "another one." See Henry Abraham, *Justices and Presidents* 3d ed. (New York: Oxford Univ. Press, 1992), pp. 178–79. Charles Whittaker, appointed by Eisenhower in 1957, served five undistinguished years on the Court. He was paralyzed by indecision, and the resulting anxiety led to a nervous breakdown and his resignation from the Court. William Douglas recounted the tale of a case in which Whittaker was assigned the majority opinion and Douglas voiced a dissent. Unable to decide how to proceed, Whittaker sought Douglas's advice. Not one to be constrained by convention, Douglas agreed to draft a majority opinion as well as write his own dissent, and within the hour the draft was on Whittaker's desk. This was one of the few times, Douglas caustically noted in his autobiography, "in which the majority and minority opinions were written by the same man." Douglas, *The Court Years, 1939–1975* (New York: Random House, 1980), pp. 173–74.

of the Washington political scene and was, in retrospect, the first sign that the constellation of political forces in the process of selecting and confirming Supreme Court was undergoing realignment. The end of the Roosevelt coalition split the Democratic party between old-line party regulars and the New Progressives. During the last quarter century the federal judiciary has become an important ally of the New Progressives in securing and protecting policy victories, particularly the lifestyle issues of exceptional importance to an educated, upper-middle-class, professional elite. The litigation victories of the New Progressives in turn hastened the emergence of the New Right in the Republican party and gave rise to intense scrutiny of judicial appointments by powerful forces in both parties. The changes in the nature of judicial power over the last three decades ratcheted the stakes still higher by making the federal judiciary amenable to a wider range of litigants and claims than ever before in its institutional history. Changes in the formal rules and institutional folkways of the Senate enhanced the influence of individual senators at the expense of institutional cohesion and leadership control. By the late 1960s these developments converged, making public battles over the staffing the Supreme Court almost inevitable.

In this context neither the defeat of Bork nor the spectacle of the Thomas hearings can be understood as aberrations. Quite the contrary, both stand as examples of the new model of confirmation politics. Robert Bork was perhaps the most professionally qualified candidate since Felix Frankfurter, but in the contemporary process the more eminent and well-known the candidate, the greater the likelihood of divisive and contentious hearings. The present reality is that prominence facilitates the mobilization of opposition. The nomination of Clarence Thomas illustrates another side of the new politics of confirmations. Legal stature and professional accomplishment were not determinants in his selection; President Bush's statement that Thomas was "the best-qualified" to succeed the retiring Justice Marshall rang so hollow as to embarrass even the most cynical of observers. His nomination represented the rankest form of political symbolism and affirmative action. The special qualities Thomas brought to the process—the support of the New Right and the fact that he was an African-American who had "made it" in America—were deemed crucial in the battle to hold public support and place a conservative activist on the Court. Between the boundaries set by Bork and Thomas are the relative unknown, "stealth" appointees—O'Connor, Kennedy, Souter—who now form the center bloc on the Court. Obscure candidates have proven to be relatively safe choices for recent presidents, but the betting here is that this strategy will soon prove obsolete. The stakes have become too high for too many interests for unknowns to continue to be given a free pass. The process of selecting and confirming judges has become thoroughly democratized, and that increases the likelihood of contentious proceedings, whatever the background and quality of the nominee.

It is in the often unseemly clash of opposing interests that the modern liberal-democratic state seeks to achieve rough consensus on its most pressing and divisive issues. Considering the developments of the last decades, it can scarcely be surprising that a similar struggle now defines the selection of our judges. The harsh reality of recent experience—that modern interest group and media politics shape the selection of judges to our highest courts—has provoked a good deal of concern on the part of politician and citizen alike, and calls for the reform of the process of "advice and consent" are frequently heard.[3] To those who witnessed the agony of the Thomas hearings, the value of a return to less visible and contentious proceedings may appear undeniable. Reform, however, is not only unlikely—again because the stakes are too high for too many interests—but perhaps ill advised as well. History teaches us that the apparent decorum of the past was achieved at the expense of public participation and accountability. One may decry the demise of civility, but the fact remains that judges today are important policymakers and that public participation in the process of their selection may be the principal mechanism for

3. See the perceptive essay by David O'Brien in *Judicial Roulette: Report of the Twentieth Century Fund Task Force on Judicial Selection* (New York: Priority Press, 1988). For the view from the Senate, consider Paul Simon, *Advice and Consent* (Washington, D.C.: National Press Books, 1992), pp. 303–17.

ensuring a measure of political accountability. That a politicized system of selecting and confirming our judges may mean that people of stature, a Brandeis and a Holmes, a Marshall and a Warren, do not find their way to the Court is a consequence that must be measured against a paramount commitment to self-rule. The modern process may at times disappoint and perhaps even shock, but the day is long past when the crucial decisions of governance are made by a small group of men far removed from the glare of public scrutiny.

EPILOGUE: THE GINSBURG
APPOINTMENT

*"The administration's process for selecting a Supreme Court nominee
needs real improvement."*
> —Arthur Kropp, president of the
> New Progressive group People for
> the American Way

*"But do I regret the fact that there were leaks and that that may have
exposed them [Interior Secretary Bruce Babbit and Judge Stephen Breyer,
the apparent frontrunners for the nomination] more than they would
otherwise have been? I certainly do. And I'd be happy to—you know, we
ought to do better with that. And if somebody's got any suggestions about
how I can, I'd like to have them."*
> —President Bill Clinton, at a press
> conference following the nomination of
> Judge Ruth Bader Ginsburg

When the hearings on the nomination of Ruth Bader Ginsburg
opened before the Senate Judiciary Committee on July 20, 1993, the
sense of relief among the members of the committee was palpable.
Gone was the tension, the air of suspicion and hostility, the expectation that something momentous was about to take place that had
marked hearings on Supreme Court nominations during the past
several decades. Republicans and Democrats were unanimous in their
praise of Judge Ginsburg; many predicted she would be confirmed by

the full Senate without a single negative vote (the actual vote was 96 to 3). The cacophony of voices demanding to be heard on recent nominations to the Court was also muted; both New Progressives and the New Right, determining that confirmation was a sure thing, refrained from mounting major campaigns to support or challenge the nominee. When Chairman Joe Biden welcomed Judge Ginsburg and expressed, on behalf of the members of the Judiciary Committee, the sentiment that they were all happy she was there, one had the distinct impression that he actually meant it.

The bipartisan accolades were somewhat surprising, because for a good deal of her legal career Ruth Bader Ginsburg personified the New Progressives' effective use of the federal courts to promote social change. The first women editor of the *Harvard Law Review,* Ginsburg taught at Rutgers University Law School before becoming the first tenured women professor at Columbia University Law School. While at Columbia, she also served as general counsel to the American Civil Liberties Union and helped form the ACLU's Women's Rights Project. In the latter capacity, she argued six major gender discrimination cases before the Supreme Court, prompting the former dean of the Harvard Law School and solicitor general Erwin Griswold to compare her work in women's rights to that of Thurgood Marshall in the realm of civil rights.[1] Although the comparison appears a bit overblown, the fact remains that throughout the 1970s Ruth Bader Ginsburg was gender equality's most effective constitutional advocate. Nominated to the U.S. Court of Appeals for the D.C. Circuit by Jimmy Carter in 1980, Ginsburg won Senate approval despite the misgivings of conservatives who feared she was a promoter of liberal causes and a champion of judicial activism.

Thirteen years of judicial service, however, transformed the advocate of judicial action into a proponent of New Deal judicial modesty. While serving on the D.C. circuit, Ginsburg acquired a

---

1. This comparison apparently had an impact on President Clinton's decision to nominate Ginsburg. See Sidney Blumenthal, "A Beautiful Friendship" *New Yorker,* July 5, 1993, pp. 37–38.

reputation as a cautious centrist on an appellate court with deep ideological divisions. Her opinions tended to be narrowly drawn, seeking to diminish the impact of the judiciary on the political process while eschewing any attempt to articulate a broad constitutional philosophy. Although a supporter of abortion rights (she was refreshingly candid on that point during the Supreme Court confirmation hearings), she also had the temerity to criticize *Roe v. Wade*, arguing in several articles and public lectures that equal protection rather than privacy would have provided abortion with a sounder constitutional basis. Expressing an understanding of the judicial role that Felix Frankfurter would have applauded, Ginsburg asserted that the sweeping nature of the opinion in *Roe* preempted legislative attempts at reform and fueled the bitter controversy that followed. In her view a narrower ruling, permitting the state legislatures some latitude in fashioning abortion statutes, would ultimately have served the pro-choice cause better, while conveying the added benefit of redirecting public attention from the judiciary to the popularly elected branches.[2]

The moderating impact of her years on the federal bench, her gender, and her religion (she would be the first Jewish justice since Abe Fortas) made her, in the words of Senator Charles Grassley, Republican of Iowa, a "Democrat that even Republicans can support."[3] Although some New Progressive groups expressed concern with Ginsburg's criticism of *Roe* and her narrow interpretation of the judicial role and although New Right groups lamented her defense of abortion, Judge Ginsburg's competence, intelligence, and professional demeanor disarmed all but her most zealous critics. Even though President Clinton had earlier expressed a preference for a nominee who had broad political experience, was well known to the general public, and had a "big heart" and whose nomination would be greeted with shouts of "Wow! A homerun"—a description not easily associated with Judge Ginsburg—many political pundits concluded

2. See, for example, Ginsburg "Some Thoughts on Autonomy and Equality in Relations to Roe v. Wade," *North Carolina Law Review* 63 (1985): 375–86.

3. Quoted in *Congressional Quarterly*, June 19, 1992, p. 1571.

that her nomination furnished the brightest moment of the initial six months of the Clinton presidency.

Whereas the actual nomination of Judge Ginsburg played to largely favorable reviews, the tortuous proceedings that led to her selection were viewed in a far harsher light. Justice White's announcement in March of 1993 that he would retire at the conclusion of the Court's term permitted Bill Clinton ample time to consider carefully the first Democratic appointment to the Court since Thurgood Marshall's in 1967. The drawn-out selection process, however, also provided abundant opportunity for intensive lobbying and more than the usual leaks and rumors. In the final weeks the White House permitted media attention to focus first on Interior Secretary Bruce Babbitt and then on Court of Appeals Judge Stephen G. Breyer, eventually subjecting two honorable individuals to the pain of public rejection and the new president to charges of indecisiveness. Whatever the merits of the ultimate choice, the process of arriving at that choice seemed more than a bit unseemly.

It began in the spring of 1993 with New York Governor Mario Cuomo's being talked up as President Clinton's ideal "homerun" nominee. Cuomo eventually removed himself from any consideration, but not before his name was prominently displayed by conservative groups in the crusade to raise funds and muster opposition to Clinton judicial nominees. Besides Cuomo, Laurence Tribe, Marian Wright Edelman, and Eleanor Holmes Norton—whose names were certain to produce consternation among the supporters of the New Right— were at one time or another cited by conservative opponents as possible Clinton choices to replace Justice White.[4] That there was no evidence that the Clinton administration was seriously considering

---

4. Professor Laurence Tribe of the Harvard Law School is the most prominent constitutional scholar advocating an activist role for the Supreme Court. Marian Wright Edelman, a former staff attorney and director the NAACP Legal Defense Fund, is currently the president of the Children's Defense Fund. Eleanor Holmes Norton was an assistant legal director of the ACLU and is now a professor at the Georgetown University Law Center and the District of Columbia's nonvoting member of the House of Representatives. Each has, in short, impeccable New Progressive credentials.

any of these individuals mattered little; by 1993 the importance of a vacancy on the Supreme Court had obviously warranted the galvanizing of opposition even before the identity of the president's nominee is known.

In early June, Clinton struggled to complete the selection process to permit Senate confirmation before the August recess. His first choice was said to be Bruce Babbitt, a former governor of Arizona. Well known (in 1988 he had launched a dark horse campaign for the Democratic presidential nomination) and popular, Babbitt had the extensive background in politics and public affairs that Clinton, at least initially, sought in his first nominee to the Court. The selection of Babbitt, a champion of many liberal causes, would please New Progressive groups, while his nomination was certain to trigger the ire of the New Right. When New Right groups and powerful Republicans like Orrin Hatch, the ranking Republican on the Judiciary Committee, expressed concern about Babbitt's lack of judicial experience (he would have been the first nominee since William Rehnquist not to have served as a judge) and conservation groups organized to keep the popular Babbitt as interior secretary, the White House quickly redirected attention to Stephen Breyer, the chief judge of the First Circuit Court of Appeals.

Breyer, a graduate of the Harvard Law School, clerked for Justice Arthur Goldberg before working for the Justice Department and serving as an assistant special prosecutor during the Watergate investigation. From 1979 to 1980 he was the respected chief counsel to the Senate Judiciary Committee. On his nomination to the First Circuit judgeship by President Carter, bipartisan support from the members of the committee eased the confirmation process. Like Judge Ginsburg, Judge Breyer quickly established a reputation for professional competency and moderation. Although Breyer had apparently failed to pay Social Security taxes for an elderly woman who did housecleaning for his family, powerful Republicans like Hatch and minority leader Robert Dole, who knew Brayer personally from his work in the Senate, continued to support his nomination. Publicly summoned to the White House to meet with the president, Breyer seemed the likely nominee up to the moment of the announcement that Judge Ginsburg would be the choice.

President Clinton's selection of Ruth Bader Ginsburg says a good deal about his own presidency and the politics of the modern confirmation process. That Judge Ginsburg is an extremely competent, professional jurist with an impressive intellect and a distinguished record is beyond doubt. She does not, however, represent the "homerun" that Bill Clinton claimed he wished to hit. She is not a public figure of great stature, well known to the citizenry and likely to alter dramatically the evolution of American constitutional law. Individuals of such stature and promise can now be brought to the Court only at substantial political cost, and in the spring of 1993 Bill Clinton lacked the political capital to make that kind of appointment. Regardless of the ultimate wisdom of the selection, the Ginsburg appointment was the product of political weakness. Experienced, competent, noncontroversial jurists with a restrained understanding of the role of the federal judiciary in the political system may be the best the modern system can offer. There are many who believe that such jurists are precisely the type who should serve on the high court. Bill Clinton was not one of those believers. At least in the unruffled early days of his presidency, he had said he wanted more. For better or for worse, however, the modern system of judicial selection and confirmation forces even the president to lower his expectations.

INDEX